FRUITS OF APARTHEID:

EXPERIENCING 'INDEPENDENCE' IN A TRANSKEIAN VILLAGE

Critical Studies in African Anthropology

Number 2

FRUITS OF APARTHEID:

EXPERIENCING 'INDEPENDENCE' IN A TRANSKEIAN VILLAGE

by

Julia Segar

Anthropos Publishers
Bellville
South Africa
1989

CRITICAL STUDIES IN AFRICAN ANTHROPOLOGY

General Editor
Frans H. Boot, University of the Western Cape

ANTHROPOS PUBLISHERS
P.O. Box 636
7535 Bellville
South Africa

ISBN 0 620 13588 3

Origination by BellSet, Cape Town
Printed by Mills Litho (Pty) Ltd, Cape Town

CONTENTS

FOREWORD

ABOUT THE SERIES

The aim of the series is to promote critical analysis of the African, and particularly the Southern African, scene. The parameters of this scene are comprehensive and include government, industry, education, sport, religion, art, communication (film, radio, press), 'development' and whatever activity and institution in which the interplay between race, language, culture, class and ethnic group is reflected. Our approach in the series is related to critical anthropology defined as —

> *an amalgamated discipline, in which scholars of diverse theoretical positions have combined analyses of a given people's mode of life and the effects on it of the political-economic activity of nation states and other 'control systems'. A loosely-knit field of anthropological expertise and concern, it draws from Marxism, literary criticism, and post-structuralist philosopy as well as anthropology and welds aspects of such schools of thought to certain traditional anthropological specialities. The features that are common to critical anthropology include the ethnography of a given people carried on through time; continued analysis and monitoring of the nation state and world system as they impinge on a given people; a knowledge of world ethnology and an ability to confront ethnological generalizations continuously with fresh ethnographic data; and a willingness to enter various literary and political arenas on behalf of given peoples caught up in struggles for autonomy, or more satisfactory ecological, economic, political, social or cultural circumstances (Seymour-Smith, 1986:57).*

The first title in the series is: *Tomaselli, Keyan* et al
Myth, Race and Power: South Africans Imaged on
Film and T.V. 1986.

ABOUT THE AUTHOR

Julia Segar studied Social Anthropology at the University of Cape Town and is currently lecturing in the Anthropology Department at Rhodes University. In addition to rural research in Transkei, she has worked as part of a research team investigating conditions of life in Cape Town's migrant labour hostels. Her present interest is in the rapidly growing field of medical anthropology in South Africa.

ABOUT THE BOOK

Much that has been written about Transkeian 'independence' focuses on broad theoretical issues and in so doing becomes de-personalised and divorced from the reality of the day-to-day life of ordinary Transkeians. This is also a characteristic of a great deal of modern social scientific writing which has presented quantitative data at the expense of qualitative material. The emphasis in this book, is on presenting a people-centred response to the broad political change which took place in Transkei in 1976 when the area became 'independent'. It has been the author's aim to present not only her own, but also various people's perspectives of these changes, as well as trying to convey some of the exigencies of daily village life.

After exploring some of the more obvious implications of Transkeian 'independence', such as the existence of a new administrative centre and a new border, the book examines some of the villagers' perceptions of themselves and others. Issues which are addressed include the internalisation of feelings of inferiority, the growing significance of ethnicity and the resurgence of certain 'traditional' customs, all of which must be seen and analysed in their own very specific context.

One of the striking features of village life is the degree to which most people are powerless and vulnerable. This in itself leads to fear and impotence and explains, to a large extent, the lack of organised resistance to the injustices which characterise life for many in the Transkeian rural areas.

The research on which this book is based was conducted during the period 1983 – 1984; 'the present time' in the text, therefore, refers to this period.

As this book critically analyses the concept of 'independence' in the South African context, it may be seen as an addition to the analysis of other political concepts dealt with in **South African Keywords** edited by Boonzaier and Sharp, 1988.

ACKNOWLEDGEMENTS

I should like to express my sincere gratitude and special thanks to Mrs Mokoena*, my interpreter and assistant, for her time, enthusiasm and friendship. She is a woman of great talent and strength of character and being able to work with her made my stay in St. Paul's village especially pleasant. I should also like to thank: her family for their hospitality and companionship; villagers, in and around St. Paul's, who gave of their time so generously, and went out of their way to make me feel at home; and Mr and Mrs Brusser in Matatiele town who were also unstinting in their kindness and hospitality.

I wish to acknowledge with grateful thanks the advice, assistance and encouragement of Mr Emile Boozaier, as well as the suggestions, comments and help received from Professor Martin West, Dr Peter Skalnik, Professor Robert Thornton and Mr Andrew Spiegel.

This research was made possible through the financial assistance of the Human Sciences Research Council, the University of Cape Town and the Centre for African Studies at the University of Cape Town.

* 'Mokoena' is a pseudonym.

NOTE ON TERMINOLOGY

Throughout this book I have used inverted commas when referring to Transkeian 'independence' and to the 'homelands', the reason being that I do not recognise Transkei as an independent state, nor do I accept that the 'homelands' necessarily constitute home for the people who are obliged to live in them. I have used the word 'homeland' as opposed to 'bantustan' or 'national state', because this term was used almost exclusively by the Transkeians with whom I spoke.

Capital letters have been used when referring to Blacks and Whites to show that these are not merely descriptive terms, but are official designations.

All personal names, with the exception of public figures, have been changed and the names used in this book were chosen completely arbitrarily.

Relatively little attention has been paid to the ideas of the ordinary Black villagers in South Africa in the context of their material conditions and subjective experience at different periods. Data about the ideas of the powerful, and the motive behind these, are generally more accessible than are comparable data for the powerless, and this is so especially in South Africa (Mayer, 1980:4).

INTRODUCTION

Choosing Perspectives — Macro or Micro Data?

My aim in this book is to give a voice to ordinary people — the inhabitants of a small village in Matatiele, Transkei — and to examine, in particular, their responses to the 'independent' status of the Transkeian 'homeland'. Transkei is one of South Africa's ten 'homeland' citzenship areas, the citizenship of which is determined by criteria of ethnicity. The existence of these rural 'homelands' forms a cornerstone of the South African government's apartheid policy. The situation of Transkeian villagers described here is in no way particularly remarkable — they are marginalised from the mainstream of South African life by virtue of living in a remote and impoverished rural area, lacking in basic infrastructure. They are also divided along lines of ethnicity which often results in anger and frustration being directed at one another and at the 'homeland' government itself, thus deflecting animosity away from the real architects of apartheid policies. This state of affairs is repeated over and over again in South Africa's 'homelands' and is usually out of sight and out of mind of the average town or city dweller.

A subsidiary aim is to present my findings in a way that is both realistic and engaging and therefore accessible to the non-specialist reader. This in turn raises certain methodological issues which I shall be discussing both here and in the body of this book.

My decision to embark on this kind of project came largely as a result of having read a range of literature on Transkei and having done some preliminary fieldwork in Matatiele in 1982. Much of the published material dealing with Transkei and its changeover to 'independence' tends to focus on broad political, historical and economic issues and so tells us little about more localised levels of response to the 'homeland' structures. By virtue of the nature and subject matter of these macro studies, much of the quality and detail of life at the village level is totally overlooked and thus our overall understanding of the situation is impoverished. This is not to say that broad political-economic analysis is not extremely important for our understanding of local issues, and naturally, any study of Transkei must be seen in the context of the South African government's policies of granting formal 'independence' to the so-called homelands. However, my focus here will be specifically on the 'grass roots' level with the intention of trying to capture something of village life in post-'independence' Transkei by giving a people-centred account of that life.

My interest in Matatiele and in the responses of individuals to the recently acquired (1976) 'independent' status of Transkei was stimulated by having participated in a project carried out in the area in 1982. As part of a wider study which examined conditions of life in rural areas, I spent a total of eight weeks in Matatiele during that year. My research concentrated specifically on food production and health care, but at the same time the issue of Transkei's 'independence', and in particular the creation of the Transkei/Natal border which separates Matatiele town from Matatiele district, was often raised by people in the course of discussing their access to basic needs such as food and health services.

It became increasingly obvious to me that the debates on Transkei published since 1976 (cf. Butler et al, 1977; Charton, 1976; Laurence, 1976; Southall, 1977, 1980, 1983; Streek and Wicksteed, 1981; Stultz, 1980) which, amongst other things, question the degree to which the region has attained political and economic independence and whether or not the abolition of apartheid **within** Transkei has benefited its inhabitants, are of little interest to individuals living in the rural areas. Their major concerns centre around the acquisition of food, water and other fundamental resources. Some theorists may stress that Transkeians have a greater degree of personal liberty within Transkei's borders than they have outside of them, which constitutes an improvement in their lives. Others may dwell on the significant loss of South African citizenship which accompanied the changeover to 'independence' and which contributes to even greater hardships for Transkeian workseekers. However, villagers themselves also have significant views about the way that their lives have changed since 'independence' which in turn provide different perspectives on these issues.

The focus of this study then, is directed less towards the overtly political structures like government and the bureaucracy at either the national or local level, but more towards the responses of ordinary people to such institutions, the way they are perceived and the way that people are responding to the new set of circumstances that was thrust upon them in 1976. Swartz (1968) points out that politics at the local level can be studied most fruitfully, not in terms of formal structures, but rather as a series of events aimed towards fulfilling public goals and the way that power is manipulated to reach such goals. Swartz is in fact very keen to stress that by turning our attention **away** from formal political structures (such as government), we are likely to discover more about what is really happening on the ground —

> *If we begin with public goals instead of the structures which strike us (the outside observers) as the basic vehicle for arriving at these goals we let more of the world into our investigations by dropping the assumptions that we know in advance the basic mechanisms of goal attainment, or at least where these mechanisms are to be found (Swartz, 1968:3).*

Swartz refers to this broader view of politics, which endeavours to transcend established and recognised boundaries, as the study of the 'political field' and notes that this approach allows one to examine a far greater range of data. Likewise, Barnes (1968), emphasises the inadequacy of concentrating on specialised political institutions at the village level, simply because so much political action is inextricably bound up with activities which are ostensibly directed towards non-political ends. Keesing (1981:294) echoes these sentiments by saying, with approval, that nowadays anthropologists are turning their attention to "fields" of political activity — "[T]hey look at the way laws, bureaucracies, and political parties **impinge on tribal or village peoples**; and the 'political middlemen' who bridge the gulf between the outside world and their own people" (my emphasis). In short, those who study local level politics are not searching for a broad structurally-based understanding of politics; they do not focus their attention on governments or **structures** and so do not place boundaries around political activity. Instead, they are concerned with processes of alliance and support amongst people and the way that public goals are pursued, ". . . 'politics' refers to events and not to structures or functions" (Swartz, 1968:2).

My own concern, however, is the way in which such events and processes are viewed and received by everyday villagers, the people who are not themselves significant **actors** in local politics, but whose lives, nevertheless, are seriously affected by both national and local political activity. Important, especially in the context of my Transkeian material, are Swartz's comments on the deficiency of studying those who wield and implement power (either nationally or locally) without considering the actions or **non-actions** of the public, for it is necessary to recognise that ". . . all cases of the effective social use of power or of the struggle for power, will require **the active or passive help of a public**" (1968:228, my emphasis).

This is not to deny the role of formal government structures in the events taking place at the local level. However, by concentrating on the formal structures it is possible to exclude and overlook the significance of much local level activity that is not necessarily overtly political. This problem becomes very obvious when discussing the work of such writers as Southall (1983) and Stultz (1980). From them we learn much about the goals of those in power in Transkei and how they manipulate their positions within government hierarchies to achieve these. On the other hand, we learn next to nothing about the nature of the everyday life of the majority of those people whose lives are affected by Transkeian 'independence'. Even Streek and Wicksteed, who claim to be able to tell South Africans what 'independence' means to some three million Transkeians (cf. 1981:Introduction), are only able to make the most general statements and consistently tell us far more about the oppressors than the oppressed. In a chapter dealing with corruption (1981:233) they expose a number of corrupt deals and conclude that "what has emerged is a pattern of self-enrichment by the beneficiaries of Transkei independence at the expense of the masses, who languish under conditions of abject poverty in a region designed to serve the interests of those who proclaimed it independent" (1981:243).

How, we may ask, are the **masses** taking all this oppression, how are they coping and do they **perceive** themselves as being **more**, or **less**, oppressed since the advent of Transkeian 'independence'? Who do they identify as being their oppressors? These questions can only be answered by studying the situation on the ground — that is, by doing detailed participant observation — and, I would argue, by analysing the data in such a way that the ethnographic minutiae inform us about the political structures rather than approaching the problems from an understanding based on ideas of structure.

This brings us to the oft discussed, and seldom successfully resolved, problem of integrating 'macro' and 'micro' level data, and striking the right balance between the quantity and quality of information obtained. Some questions can only be answered by studying the situation on the ground, for there is a temptation when discussing macro-level data to dehumanise people and speak of them in terms of 'masses', 'classes', the 'rural poor', etc. and to see uniformity where there is in fact diversity and variation. We should perhaps heed Comaroff's (1982:45) admonition that —

> *To view local communities, their structures and contemporary predicaments purely as the product of external historical forces . . . is to render them inert and vacuous, to deny them any active role in the dialectics of their own history.*

As Pelto and Pelto (1978:ix) point out, over-quantified information soon becomes divorced from flesh and blood human issues, and so strains our credulity, whereas purely descriptive and anecdotal material needs to be anchored in a foundation of context and quantifiable analysis. So "the problem is not **which** mode of data gathering to use but how to **integrate both** to build credible and effective anthropological knowledge" (Pelto and Pelto 1978:ix, original emphasis).

Presentation of Ethnography — More Than Just Packaging

Recently a number of anthropologists have addressed themselves to the problems of credibility and authority in the presentation of ethnography, which in turn pose questions about fieldwork practices (cf. Clifford, 1983; Kuper, 1980; Marcus and Cushman, 1982; Rosaldo, 1986; Thornton, 1983). I would like to discuss some of these issues here, and in so doing, begin to introduce some aspects of my own fieldwork experience in Matatiele which I shall be discussing later.

Anthropologists have long extolled the virtues of field methods which lay stress on the intensive collection of qualitative data carried out on a small scale. But concentration on the small scale and the local has often been found to be severely wanting — "[A]nthropology has been a discipline good at seeing local trees, but often inadequate in seeing the forests that lie beyond" (Keesing, 1981:8). Nowadays anthropologists are often at great pains to include wider historical, economic and political considerations in their analyses and to emphasise the need for a broader perspective on anthropological data. However, an eagerness to show that social anthropology, and the social sciences in general, are truly 'scientific' seems to lead to an overemphasis on the importance of quantifiable information. As Nelson (1979:76) points out in something of an understatement —

> *Lightning visits by teams of research assistants distributing vast numbers of carefully structured questionnaires to random samples of villagers cannot adequately explore questions of social interaction.*

Naturally, I do not deny the value of statistical and quantifiable data; just as I acknowledge the importance of placing local and individual experiences against the broader canvas of macro-political factors. However, the challenge is to try **not** to regard people as being ineluctably carried along by outside forces, but to recognise that response by individuals to similiar circumstances need not necessarily be identical. Comaroff neatly sums this up with the following statement —

> *... because economy, society and culture in the third world are inevitably shaped by a continuing confrontation between internal forms and external forces, it follows that the units of analysis for an historical anthropology necessarily lie in (i) the internal dialectics of the local systems and, simultaneously, (ii) the dialectics of their articulation with their total contexts (1982:172).*

Or in the plainer words of the philosopher, Paul Feyerabend in his controversial book — **Against Method** — "... the world which we want to explore is a largely unknown entity. We must therefore keep our options open and we must not restrict ourselves in advance" (1975:20).

In this respect, we can learn much from social historians who aim to recapture some of the spirit of the times that they are reconstructing by stressing the role of the individual in history. Elphick (1983), discussing methodology in South African historiography, argues the case for the 'liberal' historians who have come under fire from their Marxist colleagues. Briefly the core of disagreement lies within the varying approaches to historical data. Marxist analysis begins with a consideration of structural problems — that is — the class struggle, whereas liberal historians centre their attention on the individual consciousness of historical actors. Elphick draws heavily upon the work of the historian R G Collingwood, (calling his own position " 'soft' Collingwoodianism", 1983:4) for whom, he says, history was the study "not of the past in general, but of humanity-in-time. Historical events . . . are human activities" (1983:4). Collingwood himself was no doubt drawing from the work of the Italian 18th century philosopher, Giambattista Vico, some of whose writings he had translated into English (cf. Berlin, 1976:4). In the **De Antiquissima** of 1710, Vico wrote —

The useful historians are not those who give general descriptions of facts and explain them by reference to general conditions, but those who go into the greatest detail and reveal the particular cause of each event (quoted in Berlin,1976:1)

So we appear to have come full circle, with Elphick writing in the 1980s, propounding the importance of the individual actor and of empirical evidence and the shortcomings of viewing people not as "the subjects or creators of history, but rather the bearers of social relations" (1983:7). Just as Comaroff warns us not to ignore the role that individuals play in the dialectics of their own history, so here we are reminded that "there are capitalists (not just capital), that they do assess levels of production (sometimes puffing cigars around a table, sometimes alone with the **Wall Street Journal**); and that they do take action in the light of their assessment" (Elphick, 1983:10).

It is this kind of recognition and attention to detail that adds to the force and realism of Le Roy Ladurie's book **Montaillou** (1978) which reconstructs the history of the day-to-day life of French Occitan villagers at the turn of the 14th century. The book is based on the detailed notes, kept by Jacques Fournier, of the Inquisitions carried out in Montaillou between 1294 and 1324 and chronicles not only villagers' views on Catholicism, but records a fascinating account of the lives, loves, social alliances, sexual preferences and economic dealings (to name but some of the topics dealt with) that went on in the village. What is exciting about the way that Le Roy Ladurie has presented this material is the fact that the lives of the villagers appear to be **real** and **interesting**. Fournier's records are apparently brimming over with detail as to who lived in each household, how each person made a living and who associated with whom. Le Roy Ladurie has included all these details in such a way that the text often reads like a novel unfolding layer upon layer of the intrigue and gossip that characterises small community life even today. He also includes **the direct testimony of the peasants themselves**, quoting generously from direct speech, which adds greatly to individual characterisation and the sense that one is reading about real people. Like Fournier himself, Le Roy Ladurie does not simply take facts at their face value. For example, he examines the structures of authority, but at the same time poses the questions — who had the real power? and to whom did the people direct their antagonisms? Tracing lines of alliance and influence within the community he is often able to show how people, even when suffering under the tyrannies of an Inquisition, were able to outwit the authorities by giving bribes, having love affairs and using blackmail — ". . . the networks of patronage, friendship, complicity and compaternity could often paralyse the repressive force of the Inquisition in Occitana" (1978:92). This is not dissimilar to the methods used by certain people in Matatiele to ease the burdens of everyday village life under a government that many perceive to be unscrupulous and unjust.

An area of neglect in anthropological training, but one that is now beginning to receive serious attention, is cultivation of the skill of presenting ethnography in such a way as to capture the interest and imagination of the reader. Once more, we frequently find that in an attempt to be 'scientific', social scientists adopt the dry and detached tones of the physical sciences and so succeed in boring all but the most persevering reader. We have already considered the value of using direct quotations, but if we recognise also, that much of what the anthropologist says about people's actions and motives is **interpretative** rather than factual, then we begin to understand the need to supply as rich and as full a background as possible to enable readers to **picture** for themselves what is being described. Clifford (1983), as well as Marcus and Cushman (1982) compare ethnographic texts with novels in that both should address certain basic problems. Marcus and Cushman identify and review current trends in experimental ethnography which seek to re-establish realism in ethnographic texts. They note with approval the literary elements that contributed to the success of the early realist ethnographies and which are now making reappearances in contemporary work — "it is precisely these realist genre conventions that are now being subjected to diverse kinds of experimentation and in a few cases are being transcended, perhaps in the direction of a different conception of ethnography" (1982:30). They identify the most significant of these conventions to be strategically placed description, the use of plot or themes, the utilisation of differing points of view, characterisation, content and style. On the subject of characterisation, they make this cogent point —

> *The exclusion of individual characters from the realist ethnography probably accounts, more than any other single factor, for the dry, unreadable tone of such texts, something for which the essentially illustrative use of the case study (actually an attempt to sneak characterization in by the back door) could only partly compensate (1982:32).*

In the same vein, Clifford discusses the way that certain novelists are able to include the "voices" of various characters using both direct and indirect speech. He poses the question for ethnographers as to the degree to which they should use the indirect style of the omniscient narrator, thus interpreting the thoughts of their informants, as opposed to direct quotation. For unlike novelists, whose characters are their own creation, the fieldworker can never really **know** what informants are thinking and Clifford recognises this as "an unresolved problem of ethnographic method" (1983:137). This leads us to question the very 'reality' of what we are describing. Are we merely reconstructing, by educated guesswork, what we think our informants are thinking? And should we even presume to do this or should we rather endeavour just to present what we **think** the actors are doing? Kuper (1980) suggests that the realm of 'reality' is best left to the mystics, as reality can never be reconstructed and that the thrust of anthropology should rather be directed at —

> *. . . the refinement of methods, through the definition of new foci, through the increased sophistication of our models, through (above all) comparisons; and the proof of our progress is that we can explain more (1980:37).*

Perhaps a common denominator in all of these writings on the ethnographic text, is the opinion that by employing as wide a range of presentation methods and techniques as possible, the reader will be given a better overall picture of the ethnographic reality that one is attempting to convey. Thornton (1983) describes the case as follows —

> *Through effective use of textual format . . . vocabulary, appropriate resonances with other genres . . . subtle metaphors and other rhetorical strategies, the textual discourse can effectively and convincingly fuse the generalities of categories . . . with the particularities of perception (1983:517).*

With this goal in mind — the combination of general categories (in this case, politics) with the particularities of perception of both informants **and** the researcher — we are faced with the question as to whether or not objectivity is possible in anthropological research. Beattie (1984) points out that we can observe what people are doing, but when it comes to ascertaining people's ideas and thoughts about what they are doing, we are faced with a formidable task, not the least of which is that people (ourselves included of course) are often unaware of the ideas and patterns that underlie their own behaviour and social structure (Beattie, 1984:10). Is it possible, he asks, to understand the ideas and beliefs of another culture in the anthropologist's terms, or can the **reality** of other people's ideas only be understood — as some extreme cultural relativists and ethnomethodologists claim — in relation to their own culture? Beattie's reply is that there has to be an area where perceptions and beliefs about what is true have a common denominator between cultures. Thus —

> *Truth and falsity, as qualities of statements about what is, cannot be wholly relative to the cultures or languages in which the statements are made. Even though there is room for discussion as to what the minimum of such indispensable shared assumptions might be, without the 'bridgehead' they provide we should all be inescapably constrained to cultural solipsism (1984:15).*

Once again we are obliged to reach the conclusion that a broad anthropological view of other people's actions and ideas can only be achieved by detailed observation and interaction; by recognising that our categories of understanding will not necessarily coincide with those of the people with whom we are working; and that as human beings we have certain common insights and understandings. "So", says Beattie (1984:20), "ethno- or sociocentricism is scarcely avoidable, and certainly the problems posed by our ineluctable subjectivity are formidable". His conclusions do not really leave one very much the wiser as to how to proceed.

Perhaps it would be more useful to bear in mind this observation made by Malinowski during his New Guinea research —

> . . . we cannot speak of objectively existing facts: theory creates facts. Consequently there is no such thing as 'history' as an independent science. History is observation of facts in keeping with a certain theory; an application of this theory to the facts at times gives birth to them (1967:114).

Holy and Stuchlik (1983) argue that the anthropologist collects different kinds of data — information about actions and information about notions or ideas. Since people are capable of giving meanings to actions, they are therefore able to conceptualise **models** of actions and obviously these models can only be discovered by **questioning** people, rather than by observing their actions. Holy and Stuchlik suggest that no account of social life is complete without the inclusion of this **level of reality**; for while people may act in a way quite at odds with their declared models for action, this does not detract from the existential status of their models. A complete study of social life must therefore include and recognise both the realms of actions and notions and the relationship between them. This is not to suggest that a solution lies in some kind of phenomenological approach, but rather in a more balanced understanding of this relationship. The anthropologist, too, has his/her own models of reality and one of the dangers in collecting and analysing data is that of **replacing** informants' explanations and interpretations of reality with one's **own** explanations and interpretations —

> . . . we urge anthropologists to pay increased attention to actors' notions and to recognize, in their analytical practice, that these notions are constitutive of social reality and as such are an indivisible part of it . . . (Holy and Stuchlik, 1983:121).

I have tried to stress above the importance of representing different strands of perceptions of reality. This recognition acknowledges, first of all, that perceptions of life differ significantly when viewed from an overall 'macro' perspective, or when viewed from the local level. Secondly, that not only is the method of data collection important for as full and complete a picture as possible of people's social lives, but also the methods used in presenting the ethnographic data. Lastly, the reader should be allowed to distinguish to some extent, between the actions of informants, **their** perceptions of these actions, as well as the ethnographer's perceptions and interpretations of these actions. I therefore endeavour throughout this book to switch viewpoints as much as possible in the hope that, by looking from many different angles at the same situation, I shall be able to give a fuller picture of the meaning of 'independence' for those living in St. Paul's village, Matatiele.

Fieldwork in St. Paul's — Comments and Problems

As I have argued above, methods of investigation and presentation themselves profoundly influence the conclusions drawn from the data. It follows, therefore, that some discussion of fieldwork method and problems encountered should be included here and not hidden away in a preface or an appendix. Clifford, and Marcus and Cushman note that the new ethnographies often include acknowledgments of the ethnographer's presence in the text itself, thereby recognising the influence upon events that researchers themselves have. Some anthropologists have even devoted entire books to this subject, for example, Nigel Barley's (1983) humorous and frank account of his fieldwork amongst the Dowayo in Cameroon, West Africa. Barley's book is refreshing because he chooses to write about the things that are usually left out of ethnographies altogether. He concentrates upon his experiences as a fieldworker, dwelling upon, rather than concealing, the personal and in so doing successfully imparting a real feel for his fieldwork. This treatment of research as a human activity, full of pitfalls and surprises rather than something which is necessarily precise and 'scientific', contributes to the appeal and accessibility of this kind of ethnographic account. For if social scientific writing is to be more than just intellectual onanism amongst a select few in academic circles, then it needs to be readable and engaging. The inclusion of the role of the researcher in the ethnography itself goes some way towards achieving this.

What follows is a brief account of what I consider to be the most important aspects of my fieldwork experience, but I have also tried to include my own presence as well as that of my interpreter, in the main body of this book. As I have already stressed, my aim in Matatiele was to keep my field research as people-orientated as possible. During the six months spent in St. Paul's village I tried to view politics in the broadest sense as those activities involving a range of people not necessarily bound up with the formal political hierarchies. As will become clear in the following pages, the passive co-operation of many villagers and the lack of overt resistance to the local government was an important facet of the situation (in particular, see Chapter Six). This non-action or "passive help" of the public — to use Swartz's phrase — cannot be dismissed as mere apathy but has to be examined and questioned and, as I will argue later, should be seen both as a result and a cause of people's powerlessness.

Asking Questions

At first, the prospect of making progress with research aimed primarily at political issues (including questioning people about their political non-involvement) seemed rather difficult, for people are extremely wary about talking 'politics'. This caution is not without foundation, for the Republic of Transkei Constitution Act of 1976 and the Public Security Act of 1977 forbid public criticism of the President, as well as any public statements which question the sovereignty or 'independence' of Transkei (cf. Streek and Wicksteed, 1981:34-38). These laws have filtered down to the rural population via their TNIP (Transkei National Indpendence Party) representatives, so that most people will tell you that it is wrong to talk 'politics'. However, I soon discovered that villagers were happy to speak about the most sensitive subjects as long as they were not labelled as 'politics'. To this end I was fortunate to have an extremely competent and intelligent interpreter who had grown up in the area and so was known to everyone in the village and to many outside it, which definitely made my informants feel more at ease. Another advantage in this respect was the fact that I had stayed in the same village in 1982, and other researchers from the University of Cape Town had been working in and around the village in the interim. These previous research projects and the fact that no bad results had come from them, served to dissipate villagers' suspicions, so that even at the beginning of my stay people were very friendly and open towards me.

I decided very early on in my fieldwork that an informal approach to interviews would be the most fruitful method and the one least likely to alarm people. I always answered villagers' questions about my research by telling them that I was interested in finding out how Transkeian 'independence' had affected their lives and how things had either improved or deteriorated since 1976. This comment in itself usually elicited strong responses, with people often very keen to correct any misapprehensions that I might have had about possible improvements to their lifestyles since 'independence'. I always tried to structure my conversations around certain main issues, such as people's difficulties with getting over the border and into the town or problems encountered at the administrative centre. Sooner or later these open-ended discussions would turn to the important village issues of the day, which usually involved the headman or the ranger and access to basic resources such as water and fuel. After a while village rivals were keen to talk to me so that I could learn the 'real' and 'true' side of the latest story. So, for example, I was able to follow in great detail the power struggle within the village for the headmanship, the corrupt dealings at one of the local churches, difficulties experienced with the local bureaucracy, etc. Each small 'drama' served as a 'field' of political action and revealed a great deal about local politics — information which could not have been gleaned by asking direct questions.

Naturally, case material of this nature is far more meaningful when viewed against the background of — in this instance — a complicated local government structure. This includes a civil service as well as hereditary and appointed 'traditional' office bearers who owe their positions to the Bantu Authorities Act which came into effect in Transkei in 1956 (details of which can be found in Chapter One). This in turn must be understood in the light of the South African divide-and-rule policy which seeks to grant 'independence' to various 'homelands', the citizenship of which is based on the ethnic identity of people living both inside and outside these territories (cf. National States Citizenship Act, 1970, sections 2 and

3; Status of the Transkei Act, 1976, section 6 and schedule B). It is also necessary to understand something of the basic day-to-day economic problems with which villagers are confronted, and for this reason I carried out a village census in order to have a profile of, amongst other things, population, landholdings and employment figures (most of these figures may be found in Chapter One below). However, this exercise I carried out during my last month in St. Paul's, after I had spoken and was known to almost everyone in the village. I decided to leave this task until last as a result of the responses I had received to a question schedule administered in 1982. Due to lack of time we had been obliged to start the survey immediately which had aroused the suspicion amongst villagers that we might be working for the government and might be trying to take people's land away from them. Villagers with whom I subsequently became friendly, admitted later that they had not told me the truth when I first started with the "questions".

In addition to speaking to villagers, I also had extensive contact with various bureaucrats who held posts within the administration. These contacts were often made informally in the course of accompanying people to such places as the magistrate's offices, the clinic, the agricultural offices and the tribal authority offices. (I had, however, already introduced myself formally to the relevant authorities when asking for permission to do research in Matatiele, both in 1982 and 1983.) Many times I was asked by friends to help them to fill in forms — usually applications for passports or pensions — or to help take their children to the doctor. These requests were made on the assumptions that, being at university, I was better able to fill in forms, and that being White, I would receive better service. This latter perception was often well founded and simply by virtue of my white skin I was treated generally with a courtesy and respect not afforded my companions. (This kind of attitude which one might **expect** to be more prevalent in 'white' Matatiele town than in Transkei, is discussed in some detail in Chapter Three below.)

I also discovered that in many spheres being a young woman was a decided research advantage. Firstly, with many men absent from the village either engaged in migrant labour or working in the town or district, the majority of informants with whom I **initially** had contact were women. This, coupled with the fact that I had a woman assistant, helped me to establish a 'woman-to-woman' rapport which was extremely important. My women friends were at first surprised and then pleased when we chatted about such things as the drudgery of mundane household chores that are the lot of women or gossiped about men and sex. On a personal level, it was a gratifying experience when my informants and I discovered the extent to which we had things in common. Secondly, I was often given the distinct impression that men, both in the village and in the offices, did not treat me very seriously and certainly did not perceive me as being any kind of a threat. In addition, men, especially those with some kind of authority, often engaged in a liberal amount of sexual banter when talking to me. Whilst this was not very pleasant, it was definitely advantageous, and I was often surprised at the quality and quantity of information that many men 'let slip' during our conversations. I am also of the opinion that the fact that I had no transport and limited funds contributed to my 'harmless' image. Whilst not having a car was often frustrating, it did mean that I had to get buses and hitch lifts as did most other villagers. I also rode a horse (hired from a neighbour) which caused great amusement in and around the village. In this way I not only obtained a firsthand feel of transport difficulties in the district, but was also seen by others as being a person of little status and therefore not a threat. For me the importance of this distinction was highlighted a few months after my departure when a fellow researcher from UCT, working in a nearby village in Matatiele had the unfortunate experience of being arrested, along with his interpreter, and questioned for a day about his research activities. In contrast to myself this person had a much higher 'status' being an older married **man**, who in addition drove a car — symbol of wealth and rank — in the field. A police informer in the village obviously perceived him as some kind of serious threat and fabricated various charges against him.

Using an Interpreter

The use of the direct speech of informants, as pointed out above, can often be a powerful tool in the quest for ethnographic realism. However, it also has its attendant problems. In Matatiele I was obliged to work with an interpreter as a result of not speaking the local languages — Sesotho and Xhosa. I was able to speak some Sesotho (the language spoken by the majority of those around me) but never managed to get beyond very simple conversations which enabled me to amuse people and to discern when my interpreter was not asking the question that I had asked. This means that much of the direct speech that I use has been filtered through the translation of a third person (although many people did speak to me in English or in a combination of English and Sesotho). Crapanzano (1980) writes about the use of field assistants in very positive terms. He notes that sometimes when discussing particularly sensitive issues he was often grateful to be able to take "refuge" behind his ineptitude in the local language and to "exploit" the presence of his interpreter. Crapanzano's frankness in this regard is frequently disarming, for example, when he comments that "[T]he savage is, so to speak, less cowed by the ethnographer than the ethnographer is by the savage" (1980:138), a feeling probably shared by many fieldworkers, but not as often admitted. Nevertheless, although there were often times when I was grateful to be able to let my interpreter speak for me, these were outnumbered by the times when I felt the frustration and inadequacy of not being able to communicate directly with my informants in their language.

Crapanzano goes on to discuss some of the other merits of a field assistant, noting that, in his opinion, the quality of research results is higher when using an assistant than when conducting research alone. This he attributes to the fact that with a local assistant, interviewees feel that they are not alone with a total stranger, that a feeling of intimacy can sooner be established and that the assistant can enter more fully into the lives of his/her people. He sums up some of these benefits as follows —

. . .*the slowed rhythm of the meetings, the possibility of observing often illuminating distortions within the translations, the ability to deflect responsibility for questions and misunderstandings to a third, and the opportunity to discuss the meetings afterwards — an opportunity with obvious implications for the meetings themselves (1980:147).*

I must concur wholeheartedly with this last point, for I found discussion with my assistant to be one of my most valuable sources of information. Naturally, much depends on the individual in question, and I believe that I was particularly fortunate in having the services of a woman whose intelligence, sensitivity and interest in my work made a particular contribution to the success of my fieldwork enterprise. Mrs Mokoena was herself something of an investigator, who really delighted in discovering new information and was a keen follower (as were most villagers) of all the latest gossip. She quite consciously and deliberately exploited her ethnic identity in order to become an 'insider' with almost anybody to whom we happened to be talking. She is also a very good linguist, speaking five African languages, in addition to fluent English and a smattering of Afrikaans. Whilst identifying herself as a Hlubi, she would switch from one 'role' to another with the finesse of a seasoned actress, stressing her "Sotho-ness" when we were with Basotho, or the good relations that Hlubis maintain with Xhosa-speakers, as occasion demanded. (For more detail on the manipulation of ethnic identity and stereotypes, see Chapter Four.) She never ceased to be a source of information, as well as a friend and confidante and there were often times when I had to curb her enthusiasm and to remind myself (and her) that I was supposed to be directing the research. Mrs Mokoena, in fact, played a very active role in my research, bringing various people to see me, suggesting that I interview others, making sure that we attended meetings and met as many people as possible. Through her I gained access to a wide network of people, and although we did not always agree on all points, our discussions of the material collected were always illuminating. Mrs Mokoena, then, was much more than simply a translator and one of my aims will be to include and acknowledge, as far as possible, her presence and influence in my research.

Preserving Anonymity

As I have already mentioned, 'politics' is a very delicate topic in Transkei and research in this field has to be carried out with a certain degree of tact and sensitivity. During interviews and conversations with people I was often asked (and usually I volunteered) not to use the real names of informants. Hence all the names that appear in this book (with the exception of public figures) have been changed. However, after some thought I have decided to use real place-names, including the name of the village in which I stayed. I do this because it is actually impossible to disguise the identity of the place without omitting issues which would then render much of the material meaningless. For example, I spend some time in Chapter Two discussing the implications of the border between Transkei and Natal and the importance of the town to villagers — this not only identifies the district but the Maluti township as well and thereafter it is also easy to identify St. Paul's village. Given these circumstances, using pseudonyms for place-names is a rather useless exercise as has been illustrated by Crapanzano's controversial book **Waiting**. Here the author assured anonymity to his informants and used false names for both the village and the people. However, the descriptions in the book are such that the pseudonyms are absolutely transparent disguises and thus, people familiar with the province, can easily identify the village, and informants can identify themselves and others, as well as a host of personal confidences. Reviewers of the book have been outspoken in their criticism of this breach of faith which they regard as falling short of the ethical responsibilities of the anthropologist (cf. Boonzaier et al, 1985, for discussion and list of reviews). This highlights the very serious ethical problem of what to include and what to leave out of ethnography in order not to harm or offend informants in any way.

It has been my aim not to reveal the identity of individuals nor to include confidences of a personal nature. Naturally when writing about a small village community, a proportion of whose members are literate, it may be easy for people to recognise one another and for this reason, I have decided that at times it is better to sacrifice characterisation and realism for confidentiality. On the other hand, much of this book recounts stories of bribery and corruption within various local administrative hierarchies which form an integral part of the day-to-day lives of villagers. These aspects are 'common knowledge' for many Transkeians and I believe that they should be written about — a sentiment that was shared by many of my informants.

An Outline of the Book

The structure of this book is as follows — Chapter One will give a brief introduction to the research area, situating Matatiele district and the relation of St. Paul's village to other key places. It is also necessary at this point to sketch the bureaucratic divisions explaining briefly the background and roles of the 'traditional' tribal authority and the magistrate's staff, as these forms of local administration play an important part in villagers' lives. Turning to St. Paul's village itself I outline a brief history and give a profile which shows some of the economic constraints within which people are obliged to live.

Chapter Two begins to look at some of the obvious changes that have taken place in the area since Transkeian 'independence', most of which are directly observable. These include the creation of a border between Transkei and Natal and the necessity for Transkeian villagers to use the new administrative and medical facilities in the district rather than in the 'White' town of Matatiele. I examine some of the implications of these changes perceived both by myself and informants.

Chapter Three explores some of the villagers' perceptions of themselves and others, notably Whites and elite Blacks. I discuss more fully villagers' own particular brand of 'false consciousness' — their internalisation of feelings of inferiority — and how these feelings affect attitudes towards 'independence'.

Chapters Four and Five deal with two different aspects of ethnicity. Chapter Four looks at the way that ethnicity colours people's perceptions of 'independence', examining specifically the alleged ethnic bias in the local administration. I use cases which show how on the one hand these perceptions are sometimes justified and how on the other hand, they are greatly exaggerated. In Chapter Five I discuss the practice and revival of certain 'traditional' customs in St. Paul's. I stress the need to examine these practices in the specific social and political context of rural Transkei. For example, the 'betwixt and between' status of St. Paul's where villagers experience frustrated aspirations for the 'Western' lifestyle that they see promoted in the nearby 'White' town, as well as strong disillusionment with the local administration and government, all of which appear to cause people to seek fulfilment in other spheres.

In Chapter Six I hope to be able to draw together a theme that is evident in much of my material, and that is the vicious circle of powerlessness, fear and apathy which appears to be self-perpetuating. I try to show how fear and the abuse of power operate from the village level upwards to the top echelons of the bureaucracy, even affecting areas outside of local government. Only in very extreme instances are people motivated to actions of resistance, and these actions tend to be spontaneous and unplanned. This poses serious questions about future resistance in the South African rural areas which are raised in Chapter Seven — a short conclusion to the book.

CHAPTER 1

INTRODUCING THE AREA

In order to be able to understand the particularities of life in St. Paul's, it is necessary to fill in some background details. This chapter, therefore, sets St. Paul's in its geographical and historical context and briefly describes the formal structure of local government. In addition, I present data which illustrate some of the economic constraints common not only to St. Paul's villagers, but to many people living in the South African rural areas. These conditions provide an important framework for understanding everyday life in a village like St. Paul's. People are subject to particular hardships (like the exigencies of migrant labour) by virtue of the fact that they live in one of the 'homelands'. I believe that in Transkei these hardships are exacerbated by the fact of 'independence' and in St. Paul's, a 'border' village, many of these problems are highlighted. It is clear, however, that while villagers do **not** represent an undifferentiated mass who are all labouring under identical conditions of poverty, those who do enjoy relative wealth constitute a small minority.

Setting the Scene

St. Paul's is a village in Matatiele district which is situated in the north-east of Transkei and borders on both Lesotho and Natal Province (see map 1). The district, one of the 28 in Transkei, covers an area of approximately 213 600 hectares (2 136 square kms) and, according to the 1980 census (Muller, 1984), has a de facto population of 112 947 people. This figure needs to be treated with caution, as it must exclude many migrant labourers who were away in the urban areas at the time of the census.

Today the district of Matatiele is part of 'independent' Transkei, while the town which bears the same name is officially part of South African territory and falls under the jurisdiction of Mount Currie district. Barely 12 kms from the Natal-Transkei boundary is Matatiele town, a thriving commercial centre with a busy railway station that is the railhead of the line from Pietermaritzburg. The 1980 South African census gives the town's population as 992 Whites, 671 Coloureds and 1 738 Blacks and the whole of the municipal area covers 8 090 hectares including a large commonage with two nature reserves.

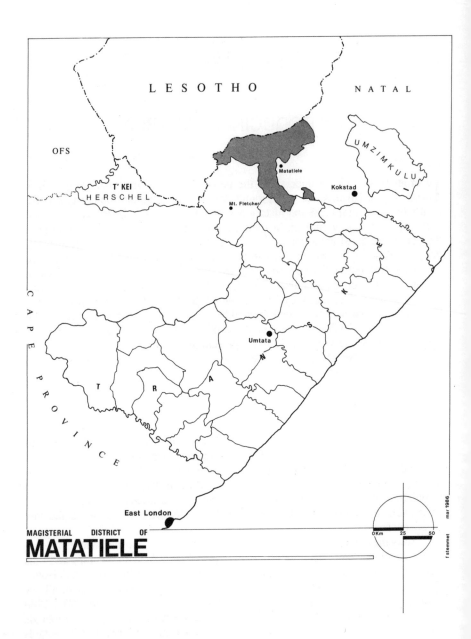

LESOTHO

NATAL

OFS

UMZIMKULU

T' KEI
HERSCHEL

Matatiele

Kokstad

Mt. Fletcher

CAPE PROVINCE

Umtata

T   R   A   N   S   K   E   I

East London

MAGISTERIAL   DISTRICT   OF
MATATIELE

0Km   25   50

mar 1986

f stemmet

MAP 1

What must immediately strike the visitor about the town is the volume of the trading activity and the number of shops, supermarkets and wholesalers which are obviously thriving in such a small place despite the present economic recession. It is undoubtedly true that the town's commercial success requires the support of the local Black population who come not only from Matatiele district, but·also from Lesotho and the adjacent White-owned farming areas.

Upon leaving the town in the direction of Matatiele district, the traveller is faced with a South African Police roadblock manned by camouflage-uniformed and armed personnel. This roadblock is in operation Monday-Saturday during office hours only. The chances are that if you are **entering** Transkei you will not be stopped, for the people who do come under scrutiny are Blacks coming **from** Transkei, who are obliged to carry a travel document. This roadblock is not, as many believe, a border post, for it is situated well inside South African territory and its ostensible purpose is to prevent infiltration of ANC guerillas from Lesotho into South Africa. (The impact of this SAP presence is discussed in Chapter Two.)

The road continues and passes the Matatiele Country Club, the local airstrip and the nature reserve as well as some open rolling farmlands. Following the curve in the road you are rewarded with a magnificent uninterrupted view of the Maluti mountains which dominate the landscape in almost every direction. You will also find that the tarred road has become dirt and that at that point, there are two signs announcing that one is now leaving the Republic of South Africa and entering the Republic of Transkei.

Here there is a fork in the road. The right-hand branch leads to Maluti, passing several villages merged into one another, known collectively as Ramohlakoana. This can be confusing for the newcomer, as Ramohlakoana is also the name of the location as a whole (a location being one of the district's administrative units of which St. Paul's is also a part. See maps 2 and 3). Maluti township is the district's new and growing administrative centre and township, where the magistrate's offices, agricultural offices, police station, post office, clinic, teachers' training college, TEBA (The Employment Bureau of Africa) and a few shops are situated. This is the place where people have to come to pay taxes, apply for pensions, passports and residential sites amongst other things. And it is here, amid potholed dirt roads, already shabby offices and queues of despondent contract seekers outside TEBA that the Transkeian government is aiming to build up a thriving township whose shops and offices will lure people away from Matatiele town in 'white' South Africa. In 1980, the Transkeian census recorded a population of 490 residents at Maluti — a mere 0,43% of Matatiele's official population (Muller, 1984). Still the government is trying to attract business people and professionals to the township by selling business and residential sites. Elsewhere in the district, Transkeians can gain only usufructuary title to land that is theoretically free to taxpayers.

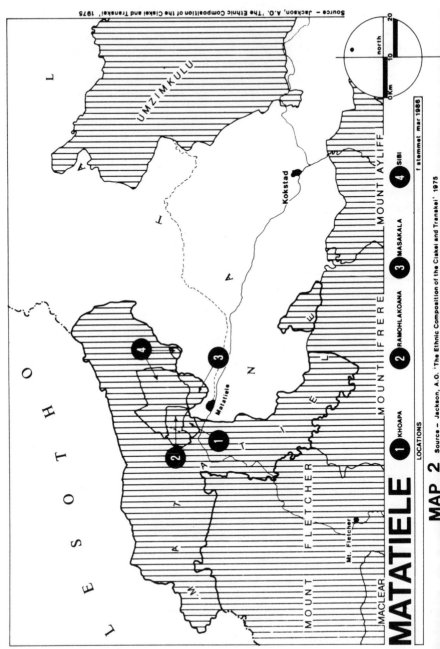

MAP 2

MATATIELE

MAP 2   Source – Jackson, A.O. 'The Ethnic Composition of the Ciskei and Transkei' 1975

LOCATIONS

1 KHOAPA   2 RAMOHLAKOANA   3 MASAKALA   4 SIBI

Source – Jackson, A.O. 'The Ethnic Composition of the Ciskei and Transkei' 1975

Returning to the fork in the road and this time taking the left-hand branch, one passes the houses of Khoapa's location on the left and its arable fields on the right. After crossing the Kinira River at Donald Drift you come to Donald's Farm. This piece of land, together with a number of farms elsewhere in the district, was incorporated into Matatiele, Transkei, and handed over to the Transkeian government by the South African Trust in October, 1983 (Proclamation R141, 1983). According to Spiegel (1985:20) more than seven farms within the district have, as yet, not been handed over to the Transkeian government. Donald's Farm has now become a military base for the Transkeian Army with varying numbers of soldiers being stationed there at any one time.

Bordering on Donald's Farm is St. Paul's, the village in which I lived and worked between December 1983 and June 1984 (see map 3). St. Paul's, as its name suggests, is a former mission station which is situated on what used to be known as Wallace Farm. The Anglican mission church still operates in the village next to the residential area. In terms of the 1936 Land and Trust Act, of the church was obliged to sell Wallace Farm and the mission station to the South African Trust (formerly the South African Native Trust). This deal was concluded in 1965 (cf. below and Segar, 1982) and this Trust land was added to the administrative area known as Ramohlakoana location (see map 3). As a logical sequel to this purchase, the area was subjected to 'betterment', a process which is automatic and compulsory on all Trust farms (Yawitch, 1981:14). 'Betterment' is the term used to refer to the so-called rationalisation policy, the ostensible aim of which is to halt and reverse the deterioration of land in the rural areas. 'Betterment' usually entails moving people and apportioning to them standardised land blocks. As Yawitch (1981:18) and others (Hirson, 1977; De Wet and McAllister, 1983) comment, this almost invariably leads to stock loss and/or land loss and entails much misery for those who are moved. Residential areas, arable lands and grazing lands are consolidated into distinct blocks which means that villagers no longer live on the land that they are cultivating. This could mean being allocated a site many kilometres' walk away from one's field. Not only does this require extra time and energy for cultivation, but also poses the problem of how to guard against the theft of produce growing in the fields (cf. McAllister, 1984:sect VI).

A drive through the Transkeian rural areas reveals dramatic evidence of 'betterment' — neatly regimented rows of huts and houses adjacent to symmetrical patchworks of fields show where people have been moved, while nearby one can often detect the haphazard remains of the villages from where people have been uprooted.

The residents of St. Paul's were moved from some Ramohlakoana villages in 1969-70 and the area where they had been living became a grazing camp. Fortunately in this instance, many villagers were happy to move to their new homes and to escape damp and unsavoury conditions in their previous residential area. An extra bonus is that St. Paul's has a reputation for extremely fertile soil, the arable lands being situated on a flood plain. The grid-style arrangement of the village, its

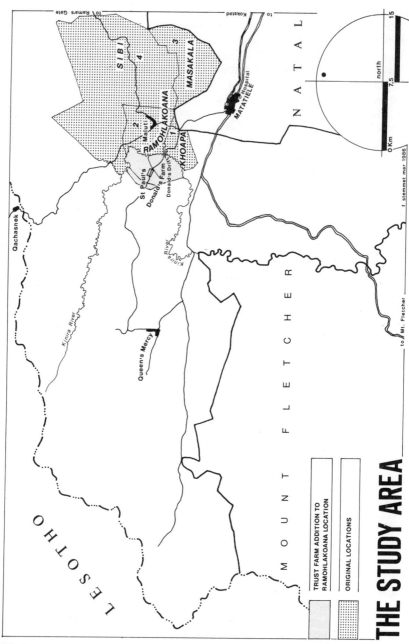

THE STUDY AREA

TRUST FARM ADDITION TO
RAMOHLAKOANA LOCATION

ORIGINAL LOCATIONS

MAP 3

relative newness and alleged modernity, as well as its position alongside one of the district's main roads, have gained it the nickname 'Soweto' amongst locals.

The architecture in the village is a mixture of rectangular and round mud and thatch huts and concrete brick and corrugated iron-roofed houses. The latter are taken as a sign of status and wealth for their owners, despite the fact that the majority of these structures do not have ceilings — usually because their owners cannot afford the extra expense — and so are very cold in winter when it is not uncommon for it to snow, and extremely hot in summer when the temperatures are well above 30°C. I was very grateful during the hot summer months to be living in an 'old fashioned' rondavel, which belonged to Mrs Mokoena and her family, but was standing empty after they had moved into their new brick and 'tin' six-roomed house. Here I was extremely comfortable having both privacy and company when I wanted it, not to mention a pleasant temperature in which to live and work.

At the centre of the village is a concrete water-tank, that is supplied by a borehole and windmill a few kilometres away. Sometimes the system is operational and sometimes it is not, but fortunately there are a number of mountain springs in and around the village which supply fresh water even in times of drought. Next to the tank is an open area scattered with a few rocky outcrops and this is where villagers meet for **dipitso** (singular — **pitso** — public meetings or courts), the men sitting on one side, the women on the other. When I first arrived in St. Paul's I was told that the **dipitso** were held fairly regularly, about once a week and that they would be publicly announced. I soon learned that the **pitso** was held when the headman felt that there was a need for one, and I never once saw or heard the village crier who was supposed to announce these meetings. However, it was fortunate that I lived quite near to the meeting place and could usually see when people started to gather.

Visitors often pass through the village as it is situated along one of the main gravel roads through the district; it is near to town and is on the bus-route and so is very accessible. A big draw-card to St. Paul's is the store — a strikingly brilliant yellow-and-green-painted structure visible from the road by day and by night, by virtue of outside lighting. Walking into the store for the first time is an unusual experience: outside there are children playing in the rutted and potholed dirt 'streets', women busy with the drudgery of fetching water from the village tank or from one of the fresh-water springs, boys and men taking cattle to the grazing camps, but inside the store there are tiled floors, electric lighting, turnstiles, electronic tills, a refrigerator . . . in fact all the conveniences of a modern supermarket. The family who own and run the store, which has its own generator, have diversified their business, owning also a large chicken battery and brickyard in the village. At Maluti, close to their Ramohlakoana homestead, they have another store and a restaurant, and were in the process of building a hotel, also at Maluti. The growth of their business enterprises has also meant that they have been able to become more competitive and attract customers from surrounding villages. To this end they have organised that their store should be a collection point for old age and disability pensions, collecting people free of charge on pension days from various spots in the district and then taking them home afterwards with their groceries, bought of course at the store. As for competition within the village, the one tiny shop with extremely limited stock poses no threat and it is difficult to see how this business can keep going. To date, no other business sites have been granted in the village, a situation contemplated with some bitterness by a couple of would-be entrepreneurs in St. Paul's.

As many accounts confirmed, land of any nature, be it for business purposes,residence or agriculture, has always been at a premium in the village. Informants described the move to St. Paul's as a scramble to attain the best sites and fields, with those in a position to pay bribes of liquor and cash to local officials having the greatest advantage. Despite the supposed standardisation that the 'betterment' scheme implies, many people in the village appear to have got a better deal than others. The size for residential sites is 46m x 46m according to the Department of Agriculture and Forestry at Maluti, but some people's sites appear to be larger than others. Also sites situated at the end of the village furthest from the road, tend to be rocky and thus of little use for cultivation as gardens. According to land reclamation plans for the area (no. T922/58A) drawn up in 1968, the size of the fields is 5 morgen (4,28 hectares — however this figure requires confirmation). Here again some people complain that they were allocated fields of inferior size and quality: for example, some low-lying lands near the river are constantly under water during the rainy period and are thus never cultivated.

At the time of research there were 162 households in St. Paul's with a de jure population of 1 206 and a de facto population of 985. Of the 221 absentees, the majority (189) were engaged in migrant labour, whilst the rest were students away at boarding school. I have used the concept of 'household' here, for although its definition is problematic, it remains the most practical and useful way of presenting statistical village data. (For a detailed discussion of the concept of household see Murray, 1981; Spiegel, 1979, 1982; Segar, 1986.) The term 'de jure' refers to the total number of household members in St. Paul's, in other words — "those who are judged as belonging to particular households but who happen to be absent at the time of enumeration" (Murray, 1981:49). 'De facto' refers to the actual number of people present in the village when I carried out the census. I have not counted as absent those people who were away from the village on short visits.

As can be seen from the table below, the majority of village residents comprised women and children and older men, the absentee rate for males born before 1970 being 40%.

However, in order to gain a clearer picture of who lives in St. Paul's and where these people came from, it is necessary to discuss briefly some of the local history. This will explain the reason for the predominance of Sotho speaking people in the village as well as illustrate the nature of the church's association with the village.

BREAKDOWN OF THE VILLAGE POPULATION
SHOWING SEX, AGE AND NUMBERS OF
MIGRANT ABSENTEES IN 1984

DATE OF BIRTH	FEMALE			MALE			TOTAL
	NO.	MIGRANTS		NO.	MIGRANTS		
		NO.	%		NO.	%	
1901 – 1910	7	–	–	2	–	–	9
1911 – 1920	32	–	–	20	–	–	52
1921 – 1930	34	2	6%	30	10	33%	64
1931 – 1940	39	2	5%	55	24	44%	94
1941 – 1950	56	10	18%	55	49	73%	111
1951 – 1960	109	10	9%	98	65	66%	207
1961 – 1970	128	2	2%	122	15	12%	250
1971 – 1980	164	–	–	134	–	–	298
1981 – mid '84	59	–	–	62	–	–	121
TOTALS	**628**	**26**	**4%**	**578**	**63**	**28%**	**1206**

From 'Nomansland' to 'Independent' Transkei

The area which corresponds to the contemporary districts of Matatiele, Mount Currie and Umzimkulu was known, in the mid-nineteenth century as 'Nomansland'. Prior to the 1860s the territory was sparsely populated with Khoisan people and refugees from the great upheaval known as the **difaqane** (Vinnicombe, 1976:57-64). The significant Basotho presence in the district (which will be discussed more fully in Chapter Four) can be traced back to Nehemiah Moshoeshoe who, with a small following, moved over the Drakensberg mountain range from Lesotho into the Matatiele area in 1859 where he attempted to create his principality at the site of current Matatiele town. In addition, two years later in the summer of 1862-3, the Griquas arrived in Nomansland, under the leadership of

Adam Kok. They were accompanied by a group of Basotho, led by Lepheana who had joined the party when Kok trekked through Lesotho.

Griqua domination in Nomansland lasted only about eleven years (the Sotho-speaking groups were also a significant political factor throughout this period) (cf. Ross, 1974). It was effectively terminated in 1874 by the annexation of the territory by the Cape government. In 1878 the Griquas took up arms in open rebellion, but the uprising was quickly and effectively quashed and in the following year a Commission of Inquiry was set up to investigate the causes of the rebellion and to evaluate compensation claims (G.72-'80). However, the Transkei Rebellion (the Gun War) took place in 1880-1 and the result was that land which had been held by those who had come out in rebellion, was now deemed to be vacant. The 1879 Commission was therefore broadened into the Vacant Lands Commission which made its report in 1884 (G.682E1). Lepheana and two of his sons — Ramohlakoana and Sibi — remained 'loyal' to the Cape government during this conflict and were thus allocated land in terms of the recommendations of the Commission (cf. G.682E2). These lands correspond to the modern day administrative locations which bear their names. Nehemiah Moshoeshoe had left the Matatiele area in 1865 as a result of conflict with Lepheana's faction, but his brother George returned at this time and was granted the land in and around Queen's Mercy (see maps 2 and 3).

The history of St. Paul's given here is taken from documentary evidence and from accounts that I obtained from two churchmen — an interview with the Reverend Richard Mantshongo, an elderly Anglican priest who now lives in Ramohlakoana; and the written account of Archdeacon Moultrie, in charge of St. Stephen's parish in the 1940s. In addition I have referred to parish correspondence from the 1950s and 1960s. (Where relevant I acknowledge Mantshongo and Moultrie by placing their names in brackets.)

In 1878, Lepheana's son Ramohlakoana, approached the magistrate at Mata-tiele, Martin Liefeldt, and requested that a Bishop be placed at the service of his community. A meeting was held on the 27th of March of the same year between Ramohlakoana, Martin Liefeldt, Bishop Callaway and "the people". The Bishop agreed to send a White priest to serve the people on condition that individuals be selected to look after the priest and help him build a mission. In October 1878 the Reverend C.D. Tonkin arrived and the mission at St. Paul's was built by the brothers — Ramohlakoana, Sibi, Musi and Marthinus (Mantshongo). During the Transkei Rebellion of 1880 Marthinus and Musi sided with the 'rebels' and fled to Lesotho, but as we have seen, Ramohlakoana and Sibi remained 'loyal', as did a proportion of their followers. They were afterwards allocated land according to the recom-mendations of the Vacant Lands Commission.

When the Commission met to hear evidence on June 25th 1883, it was recorded that —

> ... *Ramhlaquana (sic) was satisfied with the Commission's proposals and expressed a hope that the Church of England mission station adjoining him, to which he had contributed over 100 pounds, should be re-established (CMK 5/13, Cape Archive).*

Later in the same year on August 6th, the Commission visited Maclear and interviewed the Bishop of St. John's who asked for a grant to the abandoned mission station at Moitere's Kop near Matatiele. It was recommended that the church be given quitrent title to the ground on which the buildings were standing. It was noted that the church had been founded by public subscription (CMK 5/13, Cape Archive). There is some discrepancy here as Mantshongo's account implies that the cost of the mission was borne solely by Ramohlakoana. The following section of his account also requires confirmation.

In 1895 Henry Tayler bought Donald's Farm from the government. He also wanted to buy the adjacent property — Wallace Farm — but Ramohlakoana objected to the sale on the grounds that 'his' church was situated on the land. This prompted him to initiate a collection amongst his people towards the purchase of Wallace Farm. Some time previously Ramohlakoana had bought a farm near the Tsoelike River at the foot of the Drakensberg - Mahangwe Farm. Under the auspices of the government in 1895, Ramohlakoana exchanged this farm, together with the money he had collected, for Wallace Farm. Moultrie states that Ramohlakoana bought the land in 1895 for 1 000 pounds of which 800 pounds was on bond and was later reduced to 600 pounds. He adds -

> *Ramohlakoana was a staunch and generous churchman. It was he who built St. Paul's and gave the 50 acres (sic) of land upon which it stands.*

It is not at all clear though, whether the mission site was Ramohlakoana's to give or not. The quote above from the Diary of the Vacant Lands Commission would indicate that the mission was abandoned after the Gun War and was subsequently granted to the church by the government.

In 1903 Ramohlakoana died and Wallace Farm was inherited by his son, Mohlakoana, who had been a rebel during the 1880 war and was consequently living in Lesotho. So it was Mohlakoana's son, Eliel Lepheana who had the task of managing the farm (Moultrie). However, "Eliel was not a faithful steward and used for his own purposes such revenue as came into his hands". This is the reason that Moultrie gives for Mohlakoana's sudden desire to sell Wallace Farm to the church in 1910. Mohlakoana was apparently so keen to sell, and to sell to the church, that he sent a letter to the Bishop offering him first option to buy at a price of 22/6 an acre — a price well below the market value of the land. The church felt obliged not to turn down such a good offer and, as they were anxious to "save St. Paul's", sent "home" to England an appeal for funds. Mohlakoana gave the option

to buy on September 10th 1910 and this was accepted on November 15th of the same year, a large part of the purchase money coming from the U.K. (Moultrie).
Apart from "saving St. Paul's", the purchase fulfilled another "shadowy hope" —

> ... that the purchase of this farm might eventually do far more than save the mission of St. Paul's. It might develop into a revenue producing investment and thereby form an endowment for the whole parish (Moultrie).

The farm turned out to be the lucrative investment that had been hoped for. The land was let out in plots of one morgen each at an initial rate of 20/- per annum, which by 1940 had risen to 25/- per annum. In 1959, there were 295 tenants on the farm hiring plots from the church at a rate of 2 pounds per annum per plot.

The situation began to change in 1958 when the South African Native Trust approached Archdeacon Knight, current head of the parish, with an offer to buy Wallace Farm, which was situated in what is known as a 'released area' (cf. Tatz, 1962). In terms of the 1936 Land and Trust Act the South African Native Trust had been empowered to expropriate farms if owners were (or are) unwilling to negotiate. The church was regarded as being a White institution and thus Wallace Farm constituted a 'white spot' in a 'black area' (i.e. Transkei). Negotiations between the Trust and the church were concluded in 1965 and, from the correspondence, appear to have been fraught with difficulties. The major problems were that the church was determined to retain ownership of the 50 morgen of land comprising the mission and its grounds, though they were quite happy from the outset to sell the farm. However, the tenants on the farm were opposed to the sale as they felt that they would lose their fields when the Trust gained ownership.

There was strong feeling amongst farm tenants and people in Ramohlakoana's location that if the Trust did acquire the land, it should do so for the use of the people in the location. Mantshongo recalls how overcrowded Ramohlakoana's was at the time, with many families without fields. Archdeacon Knight, a local clergyman, vigorously supported the claim of the people of Ramohlakoana and in correspondence with the South African Trust, repeatedly sought assurances that Wallace Farm would become an extension of Ramohlakoana's location. Both of these problems were eventually resolved. In May 1960 at the public meeting of Wallace Farm tenants, Mr S.J. Parsons, magistrate of Matatiele, gave the assurance that —

> The intention of my Department is that when the property has been acquired it should become again an integral part of the Ramohlakoana location and its occupation or settlement or use will be planned on that basis along with the location (church correspondence).

About a year later, in July 1961, the Bantu Affairs Commissioner guaranteed that the church would retain ownership of the buildings at St. Paul's as well as permission to continue its activities at the mission. But the Trust insisted on acquiring title to the land upon which the mission is sited. In 1965 the deal was finally concluded, Wallace Farm was sold to the Trust for R61 399 and St. Paul's mission site for R1 554 (church correspondence). This opened the way, during 1969-1970, for people to be moved to St. Paul's from other villages in Ramohla-koana and for 'betterment' to be implemented.

Church membership in St. Paul's today is predominantly Anglican, reflecting the early influence of the St. Paul's Anglican mission station. Church affiliation is divided chiefly between the Anglican, Catholic and African independent churches. There is a strong Catholic influence in Ramohlakoana location as a result of the mission station at Hardenberg situated near Maluti (see map 3), and in addition there is a growing enthusiasm for the various African independent churches which tend to attract membership from amongst those who have become disillusioned with the more conventional orthodox churches. The table below shows the range of church affiliation within the 162 households in the village.

CHURCH AFFILIATION IN ST. PAUL'S BY HOUSEHOLD*

Anglican	96
Catholic	47
Independent	23
Methodist	12
Presbyterian	6
Wesleyan	3

* In a number of cases membership within a household is not uniform, with some people belonging to one church and some to another. Usually this is because second generation Anglicans within a household have married Catholics and have subsequently converted to Catholicism; or because members of a household have chosen to break away — usually from the Anglican church — in order to join one of the more charismatic independent churches. These 'dual' church affiliations account for 14 of the 23 African independent church households, while 11 of the 47 'dual' Catholic households are as a result of marriages between Anglicans and Catholics.

Ramohlakoana Location and its Tribal Authority

By 1969 when the moves to St. Paul's had begun, Mohlakoana had been dead for five years. The successor to the chiefship was his brother, Moliko, who, it was alleged by informants, allocated fields and favoured those who were able to pay bribes of liquor and cash. Moliko owed his position of power to the Bantu Authorities Act of 1951 which empowered chiefs to implement 'betterment' strategy. As salaried government officials, chiefs have played — and continue to play — an important role in the distribution of limited resources, especially land, a system which has unfortunately been particularly susceptible to corruption and abuse at the expense of the ordinary villager. Since the granting of Transkeian 'independence' in 1976 the existing structures of government, salaried chiefs and Tribal Authorities have been maintained. This system of local government has a vitally important bearing on the day-to-day lives of ordinary Transkeian villagers and so it is useful, at this point, to take a closer look at the local administration.

St. Paul's falls within Ramohlakoana location, one of the 23 locations in the district. Hammond-Tooke (1975:16) suggests that Transkeian locations were origi-nally clusters of homesteads united by kinship links of lineage. Today they tend to be more heterogeneous and serve as administrative divisions within each district. The locations, in turn, are split up into smaller village units each under the jurisdiction of a subheadman who is responsible to the headman of the location. Carter, Karis and Stultz (1967:85) define the locations as having "over the years ... emerged as the crucial administrative units, capable of arousing a high degree of loyalty on the part of their members".

During my first weeks in Matatiele I was often confused by the local habit of addressing the subheadman as 'headman' — **sebota** — and the headman as 'chief' — **morena**. Informants themselves expressed puzzlement as to why their chief was officially referred to as a headman. The key to this problem lies in the local history which I briefly outlined above. It was mentioned that during the Transkei Rebel-lion, Ramohlakoana and Sibi were 'loyal' to the government. However, Ramohla-koana's son and heir, Mohlakoana, was a 'rebel' and fled to Lesotho. According to Jackson (1975:45) it is for this reason that "Sibi's descendants have consequently been recognised as chiefs, whereas Ramohlakwana's (sic) descendants do not enjoy such recognition". (It must be noted, though, that Jackson wrongly states that Ramohlakoana was himself a 'rebel'.) As the terms 'chief' and 'headman' were used by most of my informants I shall also be using them throughout here.

The village headman is on the lowest rung of the Transkeian administrative structure, a complicated system which was constituted in terms of the Bantu Authorities Act of 1951 and effected by Proclamation 180 of 1956 (Government Gazette, 31/8/'56; Carter, Karis and Stultz, 1967:84-91). It was somewhat modified by the Transkei Authorities Act of 1965, a fact not mentioned by either Hammond-Tooke (1975) or Southall (1983). At the base of this system is the Tribal Authority, which as its name intimates, gains its legitimacy through heredity and tradition;

Southall (1983:104) refers to it as "the **bureaucratization** of chiefly power". According to the 1965 Act, Tribal Authorities comprise a head and a number of councillors including **ex officio** the paramount chief and every chief and headman residing within the area of jurisdiction of the Tribal Authority. Further councillors are appointed by the head and the paramount chief and a number are elected by registered voters within the area, but the latter must not exceed one-third of the total number of councillors. The councillors' term of office is five years, after which time they are still eligible for re-appointment. The next step up in the local government hierarchy used to be the District Authorities, comprising the heads of the Tribal Authorities and nominated representatives but these were disestablished by the Transkei Authorities Act. Regional Authorities, which represent groups of districts, still remain. These bodies are made up of a number of appointed councillors including the chiefs and heads of Tribal Authorities. Matatiele and Mount Fletcher comprise the Maluti Regional Authority and the offices themselves are situated in Mount Fletcher. It is interesting to note that the functions of the Regional Authorities which hitherto had primarily been administrative and advisory, were widened in 1982 by the Regional Authorities Court Act. Regional Authority courts now have jurisdiction in criminal and civil cases involving Transkeian citizens and exercise the same powers, authorities and functions as that of magistrates' courts. This legislation is clearly designed to strengthen the powers of the chiefs and the 'tribal' hierarchy.

It is significant to note that amongst my informants — even including some members of the Tribal Authority itself — there was a great deal of confusion about the exact composition and function of the Tribal Authority. This can be attributed firstly to the fact that the system itself is very complex and confusing with the different branches of local government in operation — i.e. the Tribal Authority, the Regional Authority and the civil service — working in very similar spheres. Secondly, communication on these matters amongst the semi-literate population is very poor — there is no local Transkeian newspaper and it is often to the advantage of office-bearers themselves to keep ordinary people in ignorance, thereby ensuring a degree of compliance and vulnerability.

The Ramohlakoana Tribal Authority (also known as the Malubelube Tribal Authority) comprises representatives from three locations — Ramohlakoana, Khoapa and Masakala (see map 2). Some people were of the opinion that the chief at Ramohlakoana chooses two councillors and that the public elect two. A similar procedure would take place at the other two locations; the difference being that the chief at Ramohlakoana appoints the headmen of these locations who in turn appoint two councillors while the villagers choose two councillors. Other people believed that all of the councillors were appointed by the government, and most had very little idea at all as to how people became members of the Tribal Authority.

Some of the confusion was due largely to the fact that a new chief had just acceded to power soon after my arrival and was in the process of forming a new council of advisers. This operation was greatly hindered by the fact that directly after his appointment, the chief, Teboho, returned to Johannesburg — for the ostensible purpose of resigning from his job — and did not come home for almost four months. Many villagers feared that another chief would have to be appointed as it seemed that Teboho had disappeared. The chiefship had not been satisfactorily filled since Moliko's death in 1979. The previous incumbent had been forced to resign as a result of mental illness after having been in office between 1980 and 1982. Thereafter his mother had held the post of acting chieftainess for two years. It was a subject of some controversy that this woman, who, it appeared, was well liked, was removed from office. Members of the Tribal Authority and those near to Teboho stressed that the chieftainess's appointment was only temporary and a real chief had to be found. They also objected to the chieftainess's councillors, one of whom was regarded as a subversive element by many. (The councillor referred to, who is no longer active in local politics, told me that his house had recently been searched by security police resulting in some of his books being confiscated.) Shortly before I arrived in Matatiele the Tribal Authority building where chief and councillors meet and hold court, was burnt down and meetings were being held temporarily in a private house at Khoapa's. It was widely rumoured that this man was responsible for the deed, and it was said of him by one old man, himself a member of the chiefly clan —

> ... he behaved like a lekgoa [white person], he wanted to abolish chiefship here in Matatiele and just have parliamentarians. The day the Tribal Authority burnt he shouted — "the devil has burnt his hell and the children of the devil are scattered".

However, he showed quite clearly where his interests lay when he went on to say that —

> to be a chief today is just to have problems because the people nowadays haven't got respect — the people in the old days respected and obeyed the chief. Today people have education and think they are clever — they [educated people] are a problem.

There were two contenders for the chiefship: Teboho, a cousin of the previous chief, and another more distant kinsman. In order to decide between the two, an 'election' was held outside the administrative offices at Maluti. This was a public affair, with the crowd that was present being asked to divide and literally stand behind their candidate — a far cry from a secret ballot. It appeared to me, and was also the opinion of many of my informants, that Teboho's election was favoured by a number of established councillors and other aspirant councillors, who recognised his potential malleability. For it was fairly obvious, even upon first acquaintance, that Teboho is a simple man who is quite happy to let others speak for him. When he did eventually return from Johannesburg, a general meeting was called, at which he merely said a few words of welcome. Others spoke for him and it certainly appeared that they had made the decisions for him as well (cf. Chapter Six below). The most important of these concerned his councillors, who it seemed were all being **appointed**, no mention being made of any elections. By the time that I left Matatiele the question of the appointment of the councillors had not been completely resolved and Teboho had once more left for Johannesburg.

The function of the Tribal Authority is both administrative and judicial. All disputes that cannot be resolved by the village headmen at their **dipitso** must be taken for judgement to the Tribal Authority and only if the problem cannot be solved here, will the disputants have recourse to the magistrate's court. Cases can, of course, now be taken to the Regional Authority court as explained above. However, people were not only unaware of this facility, but were usually, understandably, reluctant to travel all the way to Mount Fletcher unless absolutely necessary, for the road is poor and buses are infrequent. People prefer to be able to settle arguments without having to go to Maluti where fines and prison sentences can be imposed. In addition, as Southall (1983:106) summarises —

> . . . chiefs . . . also . . . assumed a senior role in the allocation of land within the community . . . Apart from being entrusted with a variety of mundane tasks such as the maintenance of location roads, water supplies, land rehabilitation and disease prevention and control, they were also made responsible for law and order, control of workseekers and unauthorized influx into urban areas, the impounding of stray stock and the dispersal of unlawful assemblies.

In addition the Tribal Authorities are mandated to make recommendations in connection with the establishment of schools and the awards of old age pensions, disability grants and licences. I found that a great deal of their duties consisted in routine and formality. For example, upon first arriving in the district the fieldworker must seek permission to carry out research and live in a village both from the magistrate and the relevant Tribal Authority. One of the agricultural officers commented to me once that his dealings with the headmen and Tribal Authority were limited to courtesies. Upon going to a village he informs the headman that he wants to speak to the people and it is then the 'duty' of the headman to call the people together. For more serious matters — like wanting to plough the fields in winter — he has to write to the Tribal Authority informing them of his activities. This is to prevent any potential conflict between the Tribal Authority and the district administration at Maluti. However, he claimed that the Tribal Authority could not refuse him permission, just as the headmen could not — "they have no power at all, the real power is there at Maluti".

Although there is an element of truth in this, I would argue that the Tribal Authorities wield far greater power than the agricultural officer acknowledged. For example, when some village women who had formed a self-help group wanted to make formal application for some vegetable plots that they had been told were theirs for the asking, they had to have their written request approved by the village headman, the Tribal Authority and the chief agricultural officer (in that order) before being sent to Umtata. Mrs Mokoena was a member of this group and through her, I too became involved as a kind of honorary scribe. I composed and typed a suitable letter of request and together with some of the other women, endeavoured to get the necessary stamps of approval. The village headman, Mr Khumalo, was quite happy with the project and the next step was to get Tribal Authority approval. The whole plan was almost short-circuited at this point because Mr Melato, the Tribal Authority councillor from St. Paul's was opposed to the scheme and refused even to put the letter before the Tribal Authority for its consideration. Melato nurtured a strong dislike for Khumalo, the pair having been rivals for some years, and this seemed to be the cause of his non-co-operation . Mrs Mokoena, being of strong will, was not put off despite Melato's assurances that we would fail, and the pair of us attended a Tribal Authority meeting ourselves. Our application was approved and was helped along by the curiosity displayed by all present at my first appearance at the Tribal Authority. Mr Melato's objections were overruled and our letter was signed. The application could, however, just as easily have failed and without the support of the Tribal Authority, people's petitions for such things as pensions or plots may never reach any further up the hierarchy.

St. Paul's — A Village of Farmers?

As I have already mentioned, bribery played an important role in determining who got fields in St. Paul's and who got the best fields and sites. During the years since the initial move of residents from Ramohlakoana to St. Paul's, there has been a steady trickle of people into the village. As is evident from the table below, most of these newcomers have been able to secure sites, but very few have fields. Of the 162 households in St. Paul's, 119 were moved from Ramohlakoana villages in accordance with 'betterment' plans (5 of these are second generation St. Paul's residents who have established their own households). Fourteen households were already tenants on Wallace Farm and were not obliged to move, and the remaining 29 households have moved into the village since 1970. The table shows the distribution of fields and sites amongst households.

VILLAGE LAND DISTRIBUTION

TOTAL NUMBER OF HOUSEHOLDS 162	HOUSEHOLDS WITH SITES 154 (95%)	HOUSEHOLDS WITH FIELDS 85 (52%)
	HOUSEHOLDS WITHOUT SITES 8 (5%)	HOUSEHOLDS WITHOUT FIELDS 77 (48%)

From the table it should be noted that **only 52%** of the households have a field. The people who are without sites are either staying with relatives or renting sites from absentees. (The one household which has two fields is exceptional in that a married man and his family is still living with his parents and has not yet completed building his new house.) Of the 77 households without fields, 51 were moved from Ramohlakoana as part of the 'betterment' scheme, while 26 were subsequent and voluntary newcomers. The reason for the lack of fields is that there simply are not enough to go round, hence the ease with which bribes were extracted during the early days of 'betterment' resettlement.

Although access to land and the cultivation of the annual maize crop is extremely important to villagers, providing an important **contribution** to their subsistence needs, people rely heavily on consumer goods for their basic requirements. (I have argued elsewhere that a cash income is vital for any success in agricultural ventures and is more important than access to land alone: cf. Segar, 1984.) The table below illustrates that half of the households in St. Paul's were not engaged directly in the cultivation of fields during the 1982-1983 season and therefore were obliged to rely totally on some form of cash income. Some people who do not have their own fields, but have cash, either hire fields from people who cannot afford the expense of cultivating them themselves, or engage in sharecropping whereby both cultivating costs and subsequent yields are shared with the titleholder of the field. The yields quoted here represent the bags of maize per household after sharing. Comparison with yields recorded in nearby Qacha's Nek by Spiegel (1979:218) show that the St. Paul's figures are relatively high despite recent drought conditions, confirming the commonly-held belief that St. Paul's black alluvial soil is very fertile.

This histogram represents the agricultural activities of 162 households on a total of 103 fields; 33 households engaged in sharecropping on their own fields, while 29 engaged in sharecropping on one or more other fields; of these 6 also have their own fields. Sharecropping for those with no field is dependent on certain resources. The sharecropper must be able to supply half the cost of cultivation, the biggest expense being ploughing and planting (R35-R45), or else to own the necessary equipment — i.e. a team of oxen or a tractor and a plough — as well as to contribute towards labour on the field throughout the year. People who sharecrop on their own field are usually obliged to do so because they do not have the material resources and/or the labour power to cultivate their field without help.

MAIZE YIELDS PER HOUSEHOLD IN THE 1982-1983 AGRICULTURAL SEASON

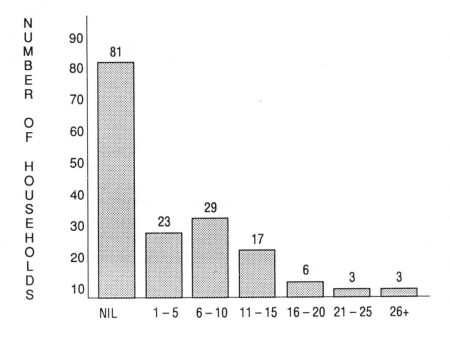

BAGS OF MAIZE *

* Note: 1 bag = approximately 80kg

Title to a field is therefore not necessarily any indication of relative prosperity, or even of potential income through agricultural activity as the case below illustrates.

Case Study: A Sharecropping Arrangement Between Two Households

The Tsekane household comprises eight people, three of whom are absent — two teenagers away at boarding school and Mr Tsekane who works for a construction firm in Durban. At home there are three able-bodied women and two young children. The Tsekanes do not have a field, but they do receive regular cash remittances from Mr Tsekane and they also have a sizeable number of stock comprising 15 head of cattle and 5 goats. Mrs Tsekane and her daughters also supplement their income by brewing and selling beer. In the

1982/3 season Mrs Tsekane engaged in a sharecropping arrangement on Mrs Tabello's field, using the Tsekane's oxen. Together they harvested 28 bags of maize and 5 bags of beans which they shared. Although the Tabellos had a field, they could not afford to cultivate it without help. Their household comprises seven people — one of whom, Mr Tabello, is a migrant. He has a poorly-paid job in a timber factory in Somerset West in the Cape. At home Mrs Tabello has five children, two under the age of ten, one son of 14 years who is mentally retarded and two able-bodied daughters in their late teens. The household has 2 head of cattle. Apart from the small remittances that Mr Tabello sends home, the family have no other material resources. They have been trying, so far without luck, to obtain a disability grant for the disabled child who requires a lot of time and attention. The Tabellos would be unable to exploit their land resource without the help of the slightly more prosperous, though landless, Tsekanes.

It should also be noted that agricultural yields are further distributed amongst villagers by the practice of paying piece-workers in kind for helping with the tedious labour of weeding and harvesting. This kind of work is very unpopular. It is strenuous and there is always the chance that the harvest will be poor and so the piece-worker is paid very little. If the harvest is bountiful, someone who has helped throughout the season, may receive up to two bags of maize; however payment is usually considerably less — in the order of a couple of tins of maize and beans (there are approximately 6 tins to a bag).

To gain a more accurate picture of the distribution of resources in the village, it is necessary to show the distribution of both livestock and fields between St. Paul's households. Apart from stock ownership, in itself being an indicator of relative wealth (at the time of research one head of cattle sold for approximately R400 and sheep and goats in the region of R40 each), cattle also represent a potential source of income as they can be used for ploughing and can be hired out to others for this purpose. Stock are also a self-perpetuating form of capital and are still an important means of legalising marriage (for some economic implications of the use of livestock for bridewealth payments cf. Murray, 1981:chapter 6).

DISTRIBUTION OF FIELDS AND LIVESTOCK AMONGST VILLAGE HOUSEHOLDS

	HOUSEHOLDS WITH LIVESTOCK	HOUSEHOLDS WITHOUT LIVESTOCK
HOUSEHOLDS WITH FIELD	58	28
HOUSEHOLDS WITHOUT FIELD	37	39

BREAKDOWN OF LIVESTOCK DISTRIBUTION

NUMBER OF LIVESTOCK UNITS*	NUMBER OF HOUSEHOLDS
< 5	43
5 - 10	31
11 - 15	12
16 - 20	4
21+	5

* 1 livestock unit = 1 head of cattle **or** 5 sheep **or** 5 goats.

Over half of the village households have some livestock, but a closer look at the distribution shows that over three-quarters of these stock-owning households own less than ten stock units each. Once again it needs to be pointed out that there is a wide degree of differentiation in St. Paul's, but that relative wealth is concentrated amongst very few.

St. Paul's — 'Betwixt and Between' Rural and Urban

The close proximity of St. Paul's to the urban centre of Matatiele and the administrative centre at Maluti, places it in an interesting position between the rural and the urban. There has been a long-standing debate in anthropology as to the legitimacy of a dualist perspective which views people who move between urban centres and rural areas as participants in two separate worlds, the traditional-rural and the modern-urban. (For details of this debate see Houghton, 1952; Mayer, 1961; Leatt, 1982; Sharp and West, 1982; Bührmann, 1984).

The situation of St. Paul's illustrates aptly some of the complexities involved in attempting to categorise a population as being rural or urban, agricultural or industrial, traditional or modern. For St. Paul's has much of the appearance of an underdeveloped rural farming community — there is no electricity, sewerage, or telephone service, roads in the village present an impressive obstacle course for motor vehicles and are often impassable when it rains. Domesticated animals — fowls, pigs, sheep, goats, horses and cattle — are to be found in almost every household, and vegetables and fruit are tended in every other garden. However, as we have seen, a large proportion of the village adult population works in major South African urban centres mostly in the Pretoria-Witwatersrand-Vereniging area, while an additional number works either in Matatiele in shops or private homes or in and around Maluti, usually in the service of the Transkeian government.

Villagers commute into town daily to go to work, go shopping, visit the doctor or go to the post office, while others are obliged to go to Maluti on administrative business or maybe to the clinic or police station. Families are unable to subsist off the produce gleaned through local agricultural activities and are becoming increasingly dependent upon, and attached to, modern consumer goods. The similarity here with a study carried out by Whiteford in Colombia is noteworthy. He ". . . worked in a field site resembling a village; a small easily defined barrio on the periphery of a medium-sized city" (Foster and Kemper, 1974:9). The community situated on the outskirts of a Colombian city, relies on the wage labour, education and health care facilities available in the city. At the same time it retains a rural flavour, with residents cultivating small plots and gardens and keeping fowls and pigs.

Thus Whiteford describes a group, marginal in both income and location, which has counterparts in many countries. The . . . residents stand betwixt and between — no longer rural peasants but not settled city dwellers with an urban ethos (Foster and Kemper, 1974:41).

The situation in the Colombian **barrio** is such that residents feel they are at an advantage — they are able to exploit job opportunities in the nearby city, whilst having the choice to engage in agricultural activities at home.

St. Paul's villagers experience their 'betwixt and between' position somewhat differently. Matatiele town and Maluti township offer little in the way of job opportunities and local agriculture is limited by scarce resources. However, Matatiele does seem to present an example of what is 'modern' and desirable with its atmosphere of general prosperity in the business and White residential areas (the same cannot be said of the town's Black and Coloured 'locations'). Vigorous advertising campaigns carried out by the local supermarkets ensure that most villagers living near the town sooner or later receive glossy brochures advertising their 'special offer' products. Furniture stores send their representatives into the district with illustrated catalogues and offers of free transportation into town in order to view products and sign hire purchase agreements. One well-known national company takes a travelling 'bioscope' around villages easily accessible from towns, and shows the locals sports films and advertisements from the back of a van. Discount coupons, occasional prizes of their products and school exercise books are distributed amongst those assembled. Many supermarkets offer credit and of course sell a far wider range of goods than are available in the Transkei. All serve to promote a lifestyle that is beyond the means of the majority of St. Paul's villagers.

Conclusion

In this chapter I have shown how life in St. Paul's is characterised by general poverty. There is a high degree of dependence on migrant earnings, and even for those who have access to land, agricultural activity cannot support the average household. The energies of most villagers are devoted to sheer survival, and although some people are better off than others, for the most part, these are gradations of poverty rather than of wealth. These are all fairly well-documented features of life in South Africa's rural periphery and in these respects, St. Paul's is by no means exceptional.

I have also highlighted some aspects of village life which are more characteristic of St. Paul's in particular. The historical material traces the roots of the village's current ethnic composition — the importance of which will emerge in the following chapters — as well as emphasising the important and positive role played by the Anglican Church. The village's position near the Transkei/Natal border also has important implications for everyday life in St. Paul's as will become clear in Chapter Two.

CHAPTER 2

'INDEPENDENCE' — FACT OR FICTION?

This chapter seeks to examine something of what 'independence' means to ordinary Transkeian villagers. The wider implications of Transkei's changed status as discussed by Southall, Stultz and others (see below), are not issues for people in St. Paul's. For them the significance of 'independence' is manifested in a host of unpleasant impositions on their lives, some of which I have outlined here. It should be emphasised that the topics that I have selected for discussion were identified as major problems, not by outsiders, but by the **villagers themselves.**

Many writers stress that the so-called 'independent states' such as Transkei, are certainly not economically independent and simply could not exist without South Africa. "The single over-riding reality of the Transkei on the eve of independence was its almost total economic dependence on South Africa" (Laurence, 1976:125). 'Homeland independence' has been described as a farce which serves only the interests of those in Pretoria and the ruling elites in the bantustans (cf. Charton, 1976; Southall, 1977, 1983). While on the other hand Newell Stultz (1980) argues that Transkeian 'independence' has brought with it certain benefits for all Trans-keians such as the removal of apartheid laws within the territory. " . . . it is a change of incalculable importance for African dignity, whose positive consequences for African pride could flow beyond Transkei throughout the region" (Stultz, 1980:77).

Similarly, Butler, Rotberg and Adams (1977) argue that whilst Transkeian 'independence' is certainly only an extension of the widely hated apartheid system, it does nevertheless bring with it new political and economic opportunities for Blacks. They concede that Transkei, together with all the other 'homelands', is financially dependent on the Republic of South Africa and so can never achieve any true state of independence. However, they do suggest that in opting to support separate development, President Matanzima recognised that more was to be gained for his people by supporting the policy than opposing it — "Matanzima . . . showed that the logic of separate development could be exploited to African advantage" (1977:32). Most importantly they express the view that 'homeland independence' gives the recipients some opportunity to bring pressure to bear on South Africa and so bring about change.

> . . . the homelands provide new and potentially beneficial leverage for
> Africans on the otherwise rigid politics of the dominant power. Such a
> proposition is controversial for it implies an evolutionary, not a revolution-
> ary, future for South Africa, a radical redistribution of power, and the use
> of some of that power in favor of Africans (1977:219).

This recognition of Transkei as a coherent whole and a country with bargaining power is clear in Stultz's work. His argument acknowledges Transkei's economic dependence on Pretoria, but states, nevertheless, that Transkei has the advantage of having been a political entity for a considerable period of time, of having government experience since 1963 (when Transkei was granted self-government status) and of enjoying 'cultural homogeneity' (save for 60 000 Basotho), and that the country is free to do "most of the things states do — for example, collect taxes, make laws, allocate scarce resources and educate and police its population" (1980:43). Like others, Stultz stresses that the beneficiaries of Transkeian 'inde-pendence' constitute an elite group of chiefs, bureaucrats, teachers and entrepre-neurs, but that — "[M]aterially . . . the lives of most Transkeians have so far remained unchanged" (1980:94).

Southall (1983:229) criticises Stultz, calling the latter's premises "profoundly conservative", although he agrees with Stultz's treatment of Transkei as a 'de facto' entity and concedes that "there can be no doubt that the Transkeian regime exists . . ." (1980:724). However, he vehemently rejects the suggestion that Transkei's 'half loaf' is better than nothing at all and that 'independence' might in time form the basis for more positive non-violent change in Southern Africa.

In response to Butler et al, Southall points out that the 'homeland' leaders are not in a sufficiently strong position to be able to put pressure on the South African government and so to extract concessions on behalf of their people. He also challenges the legitimacy of such leaders, who, he argues, in choosing the path of 'independence', have done little more than secure for themselves the material and status gains accorded to collaborators.

This kind of discussion, I discovered, forms only a distant background to events taking place at the local level. Certainly we cannot deny the existence of a new political force in the region — the Transkeian government — and that it has made certain profound changes to the lives of many Black South Africans, who by a stroke of a pen became Transkeian citizens. However, whether or not these changes have been positive and have indeed brought greater "African dignity" or the chance for "African advantage", are questions that we may ask in a specific local situation eight years (at the time of research) after the acceptance of 'independence'.

It is not possible, on the basis of research carried out in the mid 1980s, to be able directly to gauge and compare conditions in St. Paul's before 'independence' with those pertaining now. What is possible, however, and what I shall be doing in this chapter, is to identify some major changes that have come about by definition with 'independence', and to observe these changes and people's perceptions of, and attitudes towards them. For example, Transkeian villagers are now obliged to deal with a new administration, are subject to new structures of taxation and must co-operate with **Transkeian** agricultural development schemes. So although 'before and after' comparisons may not be possible, one is able to assess changes in Transkei using post-'independence' institutions as departure points. The effects of 'independence' continue to grow as the ramifications of Transkei's changed status touch the lives of people in a variety of different ways.

One of the obvious points of contact between villagers and representatives of the Transkeian government is at the local administrative centre. I have tried to characterise something of the nature of these transactions between villagers and bureaucrats and other government-paid officials showing how bribery is often an inescapable fact of local life. As for the scrapping of apartheid in Transkei, it is interesting to note that many people were more concerned with the kind of 'apartheid', as they called it, practised by members of the local elite group (known as 'high ranks' or 'seniors'). These were bureaucrats, business people and professionals who tended not to mix with poorer villagers to whom they often referred as being 'uncivilised', whilst characterising themselves as 'progressive'. This elite group was very poorly represented in St. Paul's, with only about six households being visibly **substantially** more prosperous than their neighbours. Only one person held a good position in the local bureaucracy, while the rest of the group comprised four nurses, five teachers (including a school principal) and three people with good, relatively well-paid jobs in Matatiele town (for example, a travelling representative for one of the local wholesalers). As mentioned in Chapter One, the owners of the large village store live in one of the Ramohlakoana villages near Maluti. Freehold plots are being offered for sale at Maluti and it is here, where a prestigious residential area is being rapidly established, that many of the local elite live.

The rest of this chapter goes on to examine some other areas of contact between the administration and the people. The ethnographic details are largely based on my own first-hand experiences and observations as well as on accounts of informants. I hope that they will illustrate something of the day-to-day frustrations faced by many St. Paul's villagers and in turn illuminate the material presented in the subsequent chapters.

Bureaucrats and Bribery

Since 1963, the year of self-government in Transkei, the public service has been expanding rapidly and civil servants have fast become a prosperous and upwardly mobile middle class. Southall (1983) traces the growth in numbers and in wealth of these bureaucrats, noting that this expansion is "perhaps the most visible and substantial aspect of the entire homeland scheme" (1983:176). Figures from 1963 up until 1979 show that the fixed establishment of the Transkeian public service has increased from 2 446 to 19 800 posts (excluding the police and prison services). In 1963, **455** of these positions, comprising **18,6%** of the total, were held by seconded White officials, whilst in 1979 these numbers had dropped to **170**, a mere **0,7%** of the total (cf. Southall 1983:177, Table 6.3). He goes on to emphasise the widening economic gulf between these people and ordinary Transkeians, most of whom grapple with poverty and hunger on a day-to-day basis. The increasing wealth of the bureaucratic sector derives not only from generous salary increases and allowances, but also from what Southall refers to as "primitive accumulation of capital" — in other words, bribery and embezzlement.

It is not the bureaucrats alone who are benefiting from new jobs within 'independent' Transkei. A growing number of teachers and entrepreneurs have found that their political support is the only price that they have to pay for increasing security and prosperity —

> *Three groups of modern elites, teachers, bureaucrats and entrepreneurs have been greatly strengthened in the process of political and economic development which has taken place during the last twenty years. All are the beneficiaries of the New Deal — in terms of salary, status, job mobility, training and capital. Their interests are being well served at present; they share the life style of the political elite, but they are politically subordinate to them (Charton, 1976:72).*

This supports Southall's thesis that those in power in Transkei are not merely the 'stooges' of the South African government, who by accepting 'independence' have lent credence to the policy of separate development, but are men and women who have realised that 'independence' vastly increases their opportunities to amass both wealth and influence. So, as Southall logically points out, the emergent Transkeian bourgeoisie coincides with Matanzima's support base and these are the people who have most to gain from Transkeian 'independence' —

> *... a number of Africans are finding opportunities of wealth, influence, and — in their own terms — prestige, which are available to them nowhere else in the Republic, and they are consequently prepared to accept the limited advantages that Homeland development can offer them (Southall, 1977:21).*

I mentioned above the increased incidence of bribery amongst the Transkeian bureaucracy which appears to have been concomitant with the rapid expansion of the civil service and the accompanying opportunities for this kind of corruption. This is not to suggest that bribery is a new phenomenon in the region. On the contrary, Hammond-Tooke (1975) points out that the Bantu Authorities system has for a long time provided much scope for abuse. In addition, gift-giving as a customary form of securing favours has long been a feature of social life. However, he stresses that the whole nature of these transactions has altered: in the past people would give gifts as tokens of appreciation **after** receiving favours, now gifts are given in anticipation of favours. In other words they have become bribes. Importantly he comments that — "[B]ribery has always been a part of the local administrative scene, but, in the past, occasions for its operation were limited"

(Hammond-Tooke 1975:211). Certainly in Matatiele I observed that corruption was a way of life, so much so that sometimes it was not even commented upon. For the modest bribe of a meal or 50 cents, village headmen would make sure that a case being heard at the **pitso** would be settled in favour of their 'benefactor'. Villagers would treat blatant and obvious corruption of this nature with a shrug of their shoulders, saying that they were frightened to object as it could only jeopardise their own positions if they ever needed to have recourse to the **pitso** (see Chapter Six below). The case study below which illustrates corruption at the village **pitso** was not an isolated incident. It shows how the headman was apparently open not only to bribery, but was also able to use the opportunity to bolster his rather weak authority. Villagers have come to expect that local officials at all levels in the government hierarchy are corrupt and usually explain **pitso** verdicts and the like, as being the result of bribery. This model repeats itself over and over again and characterises villagers' dealings with local authorities.

Case Study: The Violent Daughter-in-law

Mrs Mafube's case, like most which were discussed at the village **pitso,** *was of a domestic nature. Mrs Mafube is the mother of three grown sons, all of whom are married and all of whom were living with her at the time. Her three daughters-in-law helped her in the running of a fairly successful shebeen, but her relationship with one of them—Konelo—had been deteriorating for some time. Konelo and her husband had also been fighting, which had in the past been the subject of other* **dipitso.** *In fact Konelo had appeared twice at the Tribal Authority court in Ramohlakoana, once charged with having poured hot cooking oil over her husband while he was sleeping, and, on another occasion, boiling water.*

Mrs Mafube had brought the case before the **pitso.** *She claimed that Konelo was disrupting the household as a result of the constant fights with her husband and herself. When Mrs Mafube had suggested that her daughter-in-law should return to her own home for a while, Konelo had apparently attempted to hit her and had sworn at her. Mrs Mafube said that her son (who was not present) did not want to interfere as he was frightened of his wife, and so she had taken it upon herself to bring the case to the* **pitso.** *In her own defence Konelo said that her mother-in-law was the cause of the trouble between herself and her husband and that Mrs Mafube had suggested that her husband no longer liked her (Konelo). This allegation had made her very angry and was the reason for her verbal and attempted physical assault upon the older woman.*

The case continued the following day, with Konelo's husband also present. He told those assembled that he was unhappy with his wife who had, at various times, tried to kill him and was well known for her evil temper. She had insulted his mother and he did not know what to do. He said that he wanted her to leave.

All of those who stood up to speak agreed that Konelo was in the wrong and that she should comply with the wishes of her husband and mother-in-law.

However, the headman firstly declared himself unable to help Mrs Mafube because she still had various payments outstanding (these included contributions for the local school and clinic). Many of those assembled also had various sums owing and clearly the headman's statement was meant to serve as a warning to others. On the second day of the case, despite the consensus of opinion expressed, he said that he believed Konelo to be a good and kind person and that it would not be fair to ask her to leave. He added that Mrs Mafube could appeal at the Tribal Authority— but it had to be remembered that on the previous day he had threatened to tell the chief to take no notice of people who still owed money.

To many at the **pitso** there was no question that this was not a case of bribery. However, it was not clear whether the headman used the threat of discriminating against outstanding debtors in order to justify defending someone who, **by St. Paul's standards**, was clearly in the wrong, or whether he did so merely to frighten people and show them the potential power he wielded over them. Nevertheless, **dipitso** often followed similar patterns with no apparent logic in the verdicts of seemingly straightforward cases. As one woman commented — "you have to be a relative or a friend of the headman, or else you just have to pay".

A growing civil service in Transkei has meant that more and more people regard bribes as their due, a situation that has been steadily growing in magnitude since 1963. This state of affairs has become more acute since 'independence' when the administrative machinery was handed over to Transkeians and with it, even more opportunities for "primitive capital accumulation". This unfortunately contradicts Hammond-Tooke's rather naive suggestion that by vesting judicial authority in the hands of magistrates rather than Tribal Authorities " . . . cases would be settled by an impartial, salaried civil servant who would not be subjected to the pressures that invariably bear on traditional chiefs and headmen" (1975:213). According to St. Paul's villagers, the difference in the kind of corruption within the Tribal Authority structure and the civil service structure was a quantitative one — the bribes at Maluti were more expensive. These payments, especially at the more anonymous administrative centre, do not necessarily help the individual. This is especially true in the case of pensions where applications are sent to Umtata and local officials have little influence over their success. Nevertheless, people pay bribes just to ensure that their pension forms **are** sent off. One old woman who had been waiting for her pension for over two years, despite the fact that she had paid a bribe of R2 (a 'fee' for the clerk who had helped her fill in the application form), noted bitterly that —

Most people at Maluti demand bribes — even when people are looking for contracts and so have no jobs, they still have to pay. Without money you cannot survive here in Transkei — you need money to bribe.

I often accompanied villagers to the administrative centre at Maluti, and for most of them these visits were unpleasant necessities. The interior of the building itself, like most government offices everywhere, is a maze of grey corridors and offices. The magistrate's court is situated here, as well as a number of prison cells, which presumably account for the strong smell of urine that greets one upon entering the main doors. The imitation marble wall covering is peeling away from the concrete in large strips and adds to the gloomy atmosphere. Usually scores of people may be found milling around inside and outside the building, most of them waiting in long queues. For many who are semi-literate, filling in forms presents a major problem, a situation of which some clerks take advantage in the way described above. In other instances people are forced to wait in queues for hours and unless they offer a bribe, may be sent to the back of another line. Some villagers feel obliged to offer a small present as a matter of form as they are not sure just exactly when these are appropriate. In some instances people are unaware that they have been charged too much for certain services or that they should not have been charged certain 'fees'.

Pensioners too, were often puzzled as to why they received differing amounts of cash in their two-monthly pension envelopes, and many were unsure of the amount that they should receive. However, one of the major problems that villagers cited in their dealings with the Maluti bureaucracy was the fact that they are expected to speak and write in Xhosa rather than Sesotho — the home language problems of the majority of St. Paul's residents. (This aspect will be discussed in Chapter Four below.) Perhaps one of the most disquieting characteristics of villagers' dealings with the administration at Maluti was the level of confusion. At least dealing with petty officials within the village, like the ranger or the headman who are neighbours, was more familiar — a case of 'better the devil you know ...'

Ignorance and confusion are, of course, compounded by a poor education system. Dissatisfaction with school education is a common grievance amongst parents who complain especially about the conduct of many of the local teachers.

The depressingly low standard of education in Transkei can in part be attributed to the system of Bantu Education, for many of the region's younger teachers are themselves products of that system. However, there are other great handicaps as well: chief amongst these in the perceptions of the villagers, is the alleged misconduct of teachers during school hours. Complaints are numerous that many teachers spend their time drinking, carousing in town and running private businesses when they should be in the classroom. These opinions are not confined to Matatiele villagers. Both Charton (1976) and Southall (1983) refer to the Commission of Inquiry into the Standard of Education in Transkei (1973) in which many informants gave testimony as to the undesirable behaviour of teachers and the high rates of absenteeism and unpunctuality. Charton (1976:76) comments that "[T]he idiomatic description of drunkenness in Transkei is now 'as drunk as a teacher'". In St. Paul's, it was not an uncommon sight to see a few of the local teachers whiling away school hours at the local shebeens, or to find some purchasing goods at the wholesalers in town for their clandestine businesses when they should have been teaching (see Chapter Three below). "Teachers of Transkei are drinking a lot, they are like dust from cow dung" commented one parent at a public TNIP meeting. Another mother at the same meeting angrily claimed that schools were run better under the South African administration — "We do remember the South African government . . . from this government there is nothing. It's just good at demanding money from us".

It was not surprising, then, that my only informants who were emphatically in favour of Transkeian 'independence' were either bureaucrats or businessmen. These are the people who have not only benefited from Transkeian 'independence', but also, despite the greater degree of mobility and opportunity that wealth brings, have chosen to remain there. One visiting agricultural officer told me that —

> *this independence has brought improvements to Transkei because now things are easier for the businessman. In the past Africans didn't think much about opening their own businesses, but now this is happening more and more in Umtata. Also Whites and Blacks can move freely there in Umtata.*

He did concede, however, that in the rural areas "not much has changed at all". Another man, a farmer, with sizeable land holdings near St. Paul's, explained that since 'independence' the life of the self-employed businessman and farmer has improved. He told me that one can now get loans and that there are organisations like the TDC (Transkei Development Corporation) and TRANSIDO (Transkei Small Industries Development Organisation) to help one with finance. In addition, he went on to say that there are now technical schools and colleges open to Transkeians and these opportunities had not existed before.

Finally, it is important to point out that in St. Paul's the elite group comprises a very small minority of the village population and these particular individuals do not necessarily benefit directly from Transkeian 'independence'. It is not surprising, therefore, that villagers tended to express similar negative sentiments about 'independence'. It also explains why there were few occasions for antagonism **within** the village — when anger was expressed, it was normally directed towards the local administrators at Maluti. A notable exception to this was the intrusive, but temporary, presence of Transkeian soldiers in and around the village. This is discussed in some detail below.

Over the Border

During the period of my research, amongst the most graphic symbols of the change of status of Transkeian territory in Matatiele, were the South African Police roadblocks situated within South African territory on the two roads leading into the district from town. These roadblocks, as I mentioned in Chapter One, were mistakenly referred to as border posts by many Transkeians for the simple reason that they were required to produce passports when travelling into town. When I first arrived in Matatiele and travelled into town, the policemen on duty were quite casual about their duties, often waving vehicles on if they recognised the drivers, and boarding buses and checking passengers' travel documents at random rather than systematically. Some of my friends explained how, after having their passports checked, they would slide their documents under the seats to their friends at the back of the bus who did not possess their own passports. According to the popular notion that all Blacks look alike to Whites, it was assumed that the policemen would not notice that the passport photographs did not correspond to the faces. Two months later, however, the situation changed and the policemen became much stricter.

There were several occasions when I travelled into town on the bus and so experienced these police checks at first-hand. The bus driver would have to park at the side of the road, whilst all passengers were obliged to disembark and queue in a long line at the side of the road proffering their travel documents for scrutiny. These were then individually checked and each person was told to get back on the bus. If not in possession of a passport, offenders would be sent down the road to the South African passport control office to explain themselves, and would not be allowed to proceed into town. This did not happen very often because after a while, bus drivers would not let people aboard their vehicles unless they had a passport.

The purpose of this whole exercise, according to a number of Whites in Matatiele town, was purportedly to create a deterrent for ANC guerillas who might contemplate entering South Africa from nearby Lesotho. As 'independent' Transkei has a common border with Lesotho (see map 1), South African personnel no longer patrol this area, and the SAP roadblock was a response to the perceived increase of ANC activity in Lesotho. However, this particular operation seems to have been based on the assumptions that guerrillas usually travel by bus, work a five and half day week between 8.30am and 5pm, take an hour off for lunch and call it a day when it starts to rain. Although these SAP machinations gave rise to mirth amongst White town dwellers who made these observations, they were the cause of hardship, confusion and humiliation for many Transkeians. Many do not possess any identity documents and can ill-afford the expense of obtaining a Book of Life and a passport (one needs a Book of Life in order to obtain a passport) for which are needed photographs, bus fare, a day or more to wait at the administrative centre, the ability to fill in forms and often a bribe for the clerk on duty. Many people in Matatiele speak only Sesotho and so have the added problem of finding someone to act as interpreter for them, as all official business at Maluti is conducted in Xhosa. (This in itself is the cause of a great deal of resentment amongst Sesotho-speaking Transkeians; I shall be returning to this issue later.)

So, as petty and as inconvenient as the SAP roadblock appears at first sight, it did create a 'boundary' between Transkei and South Africa which effectively prevented a number of Transkeians from getting into town. In theory this should not have presented villagers with major problems because all the facilities, hitherto available in town, should now have been found in Maluti. However, most people voiced a great deal of dissatisfaction about the quality of the services at Maluti complaining that with the Transkeian bureaucracy, one not only had to pay bribes to corrupt officials, but that one could expect large-scale inefficiency as well. This unhappiness is borne out by the fact that, where a choice is available, people prefer to travel into Matatiele town to make use of — what they perceive to be — the superior services there. So apart from the attraction of a wide range of shops and supermarkets, people prefer to visit town to use the post office, see the doctors and go to the hospital. It must be noted that the post office is a very strong attraction because many local villagers living near the border, continue to receive and send cash remittances via the South African postal system. Even if the local administration is not as corrupt as villagers suggest, the fact remains that they perceive it to be so and make a direct connection between administrative unscrupulousness and the advent of Transkeian 'independence'.

One of the most significant outcomes of 'independence' and the creation of the border for St.Paul's villagers, is the fact that they now have to deal with **Transkeian** officials at Maluti instead of South Africans in Matatiele town. Apart from the fact that villagers need now to accustom themselves to a new administrative system, with all the confusion, upheaval and resentment that these kinds of changes usually bring, has 'independence'. made any material differences to the lives of local inhabitants? The answer to this question has to be 'yes', in that the new administration at Maluti impinges upon people's lives in many key areas. Whether villagers like it or not, they are obliged to have extensive contact with the 'offices' in order to obtain pensions, passports, business licences and land, as well as access to the law courts, social worker and district commissioner, etc. This contact is increased as a result of St. Paul's close proximity to Maluti, in that regulations regarding such things as business licences and health are more zealously enforced the nearer one is to the administrative centre. Soon after my arrival in the village I made the acquaintance of Mrs Matsosa, a very enterprising woman who was always involved in village affairs. When I visited her home she was just putting the finishing touches to her new outside privy — a very unusual structure, the walls and roof of which were made almost entirely of cardboard and string. She explained that she did not have enough money for corrugated iron and that the inspectors were coming round to make sure that, in terms of the health regulations, everybody had a toilet. We both looked rather dubiously at the swaying structure and I commented that it would be rather unpleasant if it were to collapse on one's head. She assured me that this would never happen as she had no intention of using it — its only purpose was to satisfy the inspectors when they came!

More onerous problems in this regard have been experienced by small-time traders and café owners who live in close proximity to Maluti, many of whom reported that things were not running so smoothly under the new regime. The most common complaint was difficulty in getting a licence, the acquisition of which, it was alleged, required payment of bribes at several levels of the administration. For the people who had licences at the time of 'independence', the changeover brought with it a new set of problems. Many in the vicinity of St. Paul's found that their proximity to Maluti meant that they were constantly being harrassed by police and health inspectors examining their premises for contraventions of their licence regulations. The most common problems were those experienced by people with licences to serve food and sell fresh produce. Their licences do not allow them to stock items such as tinned foods, tea or sugar. One woman in Ramohlakoana reported how, at the end of 1983, she had been visited by the police (and on one occasion arrested) in 1980, 1981, twice in 1982 and twice in 1983, each time having her stock confiscated and being fined between R100 - R200. She had applied several times for an extension to her licence, but to no avail, and at the time of our conversation she was in the process of closing her premises. Many small café owners in Ramohlakoana had similar stories to tell and many believed there was an effort being made to get them off their business sites now that Maluti township is expanding and there are plans afoot for industrial development and the sale of business sites. Certainly the stories of arrests and confiscations grew in number with the proximity to Maluti, and traders in the surrounding villages did not come under the same sort of scrutiny as their colleagues.

Many St. Paul's villagers found that official transactions were fraught with frustration, and a great deal of expense in the form of bribes, which do not always guarantee results. People recounted stories of how they had to pay bribes in order to pay their taxes. Without a receipt for taxes, a Transkeian cannot gain access to arable land or a residential site. Much bewailed too, is the decline in the competence and integrity of the police force since 'independence'. It seems that if serious offenders are ever arrested, they soon secure their release on payment of an appropriate 'gift'. Some traffic police gain personal income by stopping motorists, threatening to fine them for all sorts of offenses (usually operating illegal taxis) and then accepting bribes in return for turning a 'blind eye'. One man, a soldier in the Transkeian army, has acquired considerable local notoriety, by spending his free time dressed in uniform standing at the fork in the road near Khoapa's and simply demanding money from passing motorists in return for not 'arresting' them. (It should be noted that none of these officials are St. Paul's residents.)

The Transkeian Army — Protectors of the People?

The military presence in the area is a real cause for concern amongst villagers, and I must admit to having Transkeian army felt quite anxious in this regard myself. The Transkeian Army, trained by the South African Defence Force, came into being in 1975 and numbered a mere 254 soldiers at the time (Streek and Wicksteed, 1981:91). Laurence (1976:131) sees the Transkeian Army's role as being one of support for and alliance with South Africa against African nationalists — particularly those who might be operating from Lesotho. For it is Transkei's stated aim that the army should be trained in anti-insurgency techniques for the purpose of fighting the "'terrorist onslaught' and Marxism" (Streek and Wicksteed, 1981:91). It was apparently to this end that a number of Transkeian soldiers were stationed on Donald's Farm, which is to become a permanent army camp.

Villagers were usually unable to explain the presence of the soldiers; some said that they had been told that they had come to 'protect' them, while others muttered explanations about the ANC and Lesotho. One woman, whom local gossips claimed had numerous affairs with the soldiers, told me that the reason for the military presence was the proximity of Lesotho, a country which harbours a lot of "political" people whose object it is to infiltrate Transkei and "make political talk". For this reason, she said, "the soldiers must be present now that the South Africans are not here". Rumour also had it that more soldiers would be arriving later in the year and that an airfield was to be built on Donald's Farm.

The military presence had significant and very unpleasant ramifications for St. Paul's villagers and once again proximity was an important part of the problem. At one point when there was a large contingent of soldiers stationed at Donald's Farm, we would hear gunfire in the village almost every day and especially after dark. This was very alarming in itself. At times it sounded as if we were living in a war zone, but more frightening still was the fact that, on occasion, bullets landed in the fields in which people were labouring. In addition to the danger of becoming the target of a stray bullet, villagers found themselves confronted with a different kind of problem. St. Paul's became the chief source of entertainment for the soldiers who, every evening, sought liquor and company there. From the commercial point of view, shebeen owners profited greatly from the influx of new customers, particularly those few who sold 'hard' liquor — brandy and whisky and bottled or canned beer — which was preferred by the soldiers. However, the majority of women in the village who made or supplemented their living by operating shebeens sold only home-brewed beer at a fraction of the profit earned by their more sophisticated colleagues. (Home-brew ingredients require very little cash expenditure and the end product is also very inexpensive, whereas illegally sold spirits and beer fetch very high prices and thus are connected with high status.) There was, apparently, such a surfeit of grocery supplies at the camp that some soldiers sold food to the villagers at a fraction of its worth in order, it was alleged, to obtain cash with which to buy liquor.

Many young girls, some of them only 14 years old, were attracted to the soldiers' camp by the prospect of food — fresh meat and an abundant variety of tinned goods. Many young women, however, were not so keen to 'entertain' the 'protectors' and this was the cause of much trouble in the village. One morning we awoke to discover that several people's windows had been smashed during the night. This was not the first time that this had happened, but this time the scale of damage was large enough to warrant the calling of a **pitso**. It was established that each house that had been damaged was the home of a girl with whom the soldiers had been unable so far to get their own way.

The **pitso** discussion was dominated largely by the men present and in particular by one man called Motleleng. His presence at the meeting was noteworthy for he usually stayed away from village gatherings. Motleleng had the reputation of being something of a rogue and was reputed to be a successful cattle rustler — making numerous forays into the surrounding grazing areas, rounding up other people's livestock and then taking them to Maluti and collecting a sizable reward. His wife's reputation was also somewhat blackened — it was said that she 'entertained' soldiers in her home for a fee, and was finding this pastime to be extremely lucrative. It was not too surprising then, that Motleleng argued vociferously in favour of the soldiers staying, saying that on no account should they be reported — this attitude no doubt reflecting the vested interests of his household. In the end the disgruntled women were shouted down by the men, who concluded that the responsibility for the window-breaking episodes lay with the women themselves who had "encouraged" the soldiers in the first place.

Like Motleleng and his wife, not everyone was suspicious and frightened of the soldiers. Pulane, a young woman in her twenties, spoke enthusiastically about her soldier boyfriend. Not only was he a constant source of groceries, ranging from fresh produce to luxury goods like cases of mayonnaise and tinned meat, but would invite her over on weekends to show her how to shoot and use a variety of weapons including hand-grenades. She told me that she really liked shooting, although she did not like the noise too much and was even considering joining the army herself. "Soldiers are very kind," she said, "only some of them get silly when they are drunk — then they start stealing things, raping girls and threatening to shoot people. People should treat soldiers nicely because they are the protectors of the people. They are patrolling at night to make sure there are no bad people around". Pulane was rather disappointed when I declined her offer to take me on a visit to the soldiers' camp. She felt sure that I would be able to get over my ungrounded fear of guns once I learnt how to shoot! However, I, and many other villagers, persisted in feeling uneasy about our military neighbours.

The immediate problem of the military camp was temporarily solved for St. Paul's villagers when the majority of soldiers departed from Donald's Farm leaving only a few of their colleagues behind, and the shooting practice then stopped. Their departure followed an incident in which one soldier died when the grocery supply-truck, in which he and another were travelling, crashed into the Kinira River at Donald's Drift. The vehicle must have been travelling at high speed as it broke through the metal railings on the low bridge, plunging the truck into less than a metre of water. Villagers commented that their neighbours at Khoapa's location (situated downstream from the crash) were supplied with groceries for some time as the truck's load floated down the Kinira to them.

The St. Paul's Agricultural Scheme

So far we have looked at some changes that Transkeian 'independence' has brought to the area and the observable impact that these have had upon villagers. Now I would like to turn our attention towards something that is happening within St. Paul's itself — that is the introduction, in 1983, of a government agricultural scheme. The scheme is being run by the Transkei Agricultural Corporation (TRACOR), a statutory body set up in 1981 which aims to develop Transkei's agricultural potential through the establishment of community farming projects; commercial farming projects; loans to farmers; the training of local people in agricultural techniques; the promotion of private investments as well as encouragement of agro-industries (Ellis-Jones, 1985). TRACOR claims to recognise the importance of the participation and involvement of rural people themselves in community-based agricultural schemes, but to this end they seek only to consult and work with local tribal authorities. However, as Cloete (1985:9) points out — "[T]he role of the tribal authorities as the agents of an oppressive government structure coupled with frequent abuse of power and corruption conflicts with the requirements of an effective mobilisation for rural development". After having done a study of several TRACOR maize production schemes in Transkei, Cloete describes how most people are never consulted about participation in schemes and in places where meetings **were** held — "the highly technical nature of the projects made it very difficult for people to do much more than accept what TRACOR told them" (Cloete, 1985:10). TRACOR schemes are only carried out in villages that have already been subjected to 'betterment', for the way that arable lands are consolidated into large blocks makes the application of mechanised farming simpler. The introduction of this kind of farming is one of the aims of the Corporation. As Ellis-Jones states — "[M]odern production methods involving mechanisation, hybrid seed, fertilisers and chemical control of weeds and pests have been introduced . . . " (1985:3). This stress on mechanisation and commercialisation in rural areas where people cultivate land in order to try to meet subsistence needs, together with 'the lack of consultation and communication has led, in Cloete's words — "... to a lack of any perception of a joint enterprise ... The villagers express it in terms of an uneasy feeling that they have lost control over their lands and that this may be the prelude to total dispossession" (1985:15).

The aim of the scheme in St. Paul's, according to one of the agricultural officers involved, is to make an example of good farming methods and show how yields per field will rise thereafter. St. Paul's was selected for the scheme because of the richness of the soil, the flatness of the land and the proximity of the block of fields chosen, to the river which is to serve as the source of irrigation. At the time of research, progress was slow, the construction of the irrigation dam was running behind schedule and equipment was lacking. Presently there are 24 members of the scheme, only half of whom live in St. Paul's, the remainder being resident in neighbouring villages some kilometres away. This is as a result of 'betterment' planning which has consolidated arable, residential and grazing areas. In 1969-70 when people were moved from some Ramohlakoana villages, not all of them came to St. Paul's, many were moved to other nearby Ramohlakoana villages. Some of the residents of these other villages are title-holders of fields at St. Paul's. Scheme members were chosen because their fields happen to run in a line near the irrigation dam. They were given no choice about their membership and are obliged to participate or else to hire out their field to somebody else.

As a scheme-member one must pay for ploughing, planting, harrowing and weeding with government equipment and purchase seed, fertiliser and stalk-borer control. When the irrigation pump is eventually operational, irrigation will be free. The costs in 1984 were as follows —

COSTS PER FIELD FOR SCHEME MEMBERS

Ploughing	R35
Planting	R10
Harrowing	R 6
Weeding	R 8
Fertiliser	R12,37 per bag (8 bags per field)
Stalk-borer control	R10 per bag (1 bag per field)

For many, these expenses are a great imposition. Normally one might have an arrangement with a neighbour to share the costs of hiring equipment, and operations like weeding are usually done by hand to avoid further cash outlay. As for the biggest expense — fertiliser — locals regard St. Paul's to be a particularly fertile area and deem the use of fertiliser to be unnecessary. Evidence for the claim that St. Paul's soil is of superior quality compared to that found in other villages nearby, can be illustrated by comparing the maize yields for the 1980/81 season recorded by Spiegel in a neighbouring 'betterment' village and those recorded by me for St. Paul's during the same period. The average number of bags of grain per field reported by Spiegel from a sample of villagers, many of whom used fertiliser, was 4,2 — whereas in St. Paul's amongst a similar sample where only one person had used fertiliser, the average yield was 6,4 bags (Spiegel, pers comm; Segar, 1984).

Fortunately, an understanding agricultural officer allows people to purchase less than their quota of fertiliser, which he applies to a portion of their field so that they will be able to see the difference in quality when the crop is harvested. This particular agricultural officer, Mr Nokolonzi, tries to foster good relations with villagers and create channels of communication. Although he is a Xhosa-speaker himself, he grew up in the district and speaks fluent Sesotho, which (unlike some government officials) he is not reluctant to use. He is popular amongst villagers who recognise him as an honest and fair man, but one who does not have much power.

Being also a good English-speaker, Mr Nokolonzi would often come and visit me for a chat and a cup of tea, when business brought him to St. Paul's. Conversation often turned to the problems of his job, one of the major ones being the need for communication. His only means of transportation during that period, was a horse, and he did not have the time to go around advising each member of the scheme about the meetings which he tried to hold regularly. (We have to remember that the scheme members are scattered in a number of Ramohlakoana villages.) So, these meetings, designed to explain agricultural techniques and the aims of the scheme, would often be poorly attended.

So far, understandably, there is a great deal of resentment towards the scheme from certain members, and it would seem that the technology is, as yet, not having the desired results. Despite the efforts of Mr Nokolonzi, people are not fully aware of the problems involved and do not understand the rationale behind the exercise. One woman told me of her experiences as follows —

> *My field was close to the house of the scheme — that's how I got to be a member, I didn't choose. It was really horrible this year because when the mealies were high they brought the weeder and tractor and many of the mealies were broken and the machine pulled up beans as well as weeds. We are not happy with this scheme — we are still paying from last year and now there is another big account.*

However, a few individuals **have** benefited from the scheme, and through some of the new techniques, have learned how to become more productive. These are people who were able to invest money in their agricultural venture, and this message was conveyed quite clearly at the St. Paul's 'Farmer's Day' meeting, when fields in the scheme were judged and people were treated to a series of lectures on farming techniques.

The TRACOR scheme was regarded by most of its members as an unpleasant manifestation of Transkeian 'independence' as was the 'Farmer's Day', the aim of which was to emphasise the benefits of the scheme to all St. Paul's villagers.

'Farmer's Day' at St. Paul's

St. Paul's 'Farmer's Day' was the title printed on the typed programmes that were distributed to a number of 'high rank' guests at the meeting. These included some local teachers and visiting agricultural officers as well as Mrs Mokoena and myself. The affair took place in the local school from which the children had been sent out for the day. The main classroom, in which we sat, comprised a large room filled with backless benches and a teacher's table and chair. The children were obliged to hang around outside as they had to sing to us at the beginning and end of the meeting. As it turned out, the choral performances were regarded by most as the best part of the programme and received enthusiastic applause.

A band of agricultural officers addressed about 70 villagers for five hours, during which time people were exhorted to spend money (which most of them did not have, of course) on a whole range of farming equipment and accessories. The meeting began with a display of the prize mealies from the best field in the scheme. The owner of the mealies was called upon to tell the story of her success. It must be added, at this point, that both the woman and her husband hold top positions in the local civil service and are recognised as being one of the wealthiest families in the village. The woman told us that use of weed-killer had been the key to her success, and she did not endear herself to her audience by commenting that weed-killer had enabled her to sit at home and watch other people go off to do their hard work of hoeing.

The gathering was told that the weed-killer in question cost R10,42 for 1 litre, which when diluted, serves an area of two acres. Furthermore it is necessary to purchase a spray applicator in order to use the chemicals and this costs an additional R89. Not very expensive, everyone was told in response to their gasps of horror, because it lasts for years and saves plenty of time. This is no doubt true, but is not a very persuasive argument for people whose monthly income is often well below R89.

The meeting continued with lectures on subjects like soil preparation and raising chickens. Amongst other things we were told **not** to use kraal manure, which is "useless", but to buy fertiliser, after first assessing the quality of one's soil by sending a sample of it to Umtata. On the subject of chickens, it was learned that free-range chickens are "next to useless" and a lecture was given on how to build a chicken run the "correct" way with a feeder and water dispensing gadget. Advice was given on the kind of chickens to purchase from the government and then the different kinds of feeds and mashes that should be bought and administered.

In the summing up speech of the day people were told that they were lazy, which was the reason they had not been able to produce mealies like the ones we had seen earlier. "This problem of poverty and struggling can only be overcome by combatting laziness!" it was proclaimed by the last speech-maker of the day.

When considering that most households' top priority is to seek and ensure a regular source of cash income, and that up until now yields have only been sufficient to **supplement** food requirements (cf. Segar, 1982; 1984), it seems highly inappropriate even to refer to people as 'farmers' and to dare to suggest methods and techniques, the cost of which are clearly beyond the reach of all but a very few. The villagers who had attended the meeting later commented that the lectures were for wealthy people like Mrs X and Mr Y but were not for poor people like themselves. An additional problem was caused by the fact that the meeting was conducted almost exclusively in Xhosa, while the majority of the audience (comprising largely of older people) could only speak Sesotho, so non-communication could not have been more acute. Many people afterwards jokingly told me that they would have understood more if the speakers had addressed them in English.

The whole episode was something of an ordeal for most people, myself and Mrs Mokoena included. The master of ceremonies insisted that the two of us sit at the front with the agricultural officers and teachers, which gave us no opportunity to slip outside for a stretch and a breath of fresh air as many of the others were doing. Others succumbed to fitful dozing, although sleep was made difficult because of the extreme discomfort of the seating. The final songs from the children roused people from their various states of slumber — one song was about the local bus and its route from Matatiele town, past Khoapa's over the hill to 'Soweto' and on to villages called Mapfontein and Mabua. The other was a song, always rendered in one or other version at every large public gathering I attended, which praised K D (Matanzima), the one who rules over Transkei doing everything for his people and giving them everything.

When we eventually filed wearily out of the school, the visiting agricultural officers were taken to someone's house for refreshments and were treated to what, by village standards, was a sumptuous meal. They ate first and separately as befitting their 'high rank'; the women who had organised the meal ate afterwards in another room but as usually happened there was not quite enough food to go around for the 'lowest' people. This distinction between low and high rank was a feature of life that characterised many public activities in Matatiele and led many villagers to refer to it as 'apartheid'.

Later one villager who has a job attached to the agricultural office commented on the 'Farmer's Day' meeting by saying —

> *People cannot afford to pay for all those things [referring to equipment and chemicals] . . . maybe if some of the rich ones could buy them and help the others . . . But always these high rank people are very selfish and only like the high position for themselves. Mrs X would never buy those things [the weed killer sprays] to share with other people. She only wants the top position for herself.*

As for the agricultural scheme itself, the strategies used appear to be highly objectionable. Villagers were not consulted in any way as to their needs, nor about the planning, or even whether they wanted such a scheme. Twenty-four landholders have been told they are members whether they like it or not, and so far the cash outlay for most individuals has not been rewarded by a proportionate increase in yield. Possibly the most advantageous aspect of the scheme will be access to water via the irrigation pump, but this is not operational yet and will only be available to those whose fields are nearest the dam. The choice of St. Paul's for this scheme is also somewhat questionable. It seems to have been selected primarily **because** it is a fertile area and is near the river and so will make a very good show case, rather than benefit the village as a whole. As it stands, the scheme benefits a few people who do not particularly need much assistance and the approach of those who ran the St. Paul's 'Farmer's Day' appeared to be geared towards a totally different kind of audience than was present. There seems to be little point in advising people in skills and techniques that are absolutely inappropriate to their circumstances, no matter how useful they are in theory. It was as though the agricultural personnel present were foreigners speaking — in more ways than one — a foreign language. In fact it was a sad indictment to learn from a TRACOR official at a later date that the techniques and theories behind the St. Paul's agricultural scheme had been imported from Austria along with a lot of agricultural equipment.

Problems with Health-Care

Finally, I would like to discuss some of the difficulties experienced by villagers seeking health-care and to illustrate how the 'independent' status of the Transkei affects the situation. As was mentioned in Chapter One, many people choose to make the journey into Matatiele town to avail themselves of the facilities there. Not least amongst the attractions are the six private doctors, four of whom practise together and all of them run clinics specifically for Black patients. These consultations, which usually last for a couple of minutes, cost from R8 upwards and include the dispensing of medicines. Also, as there are no dentists in the area, the only relief for toothache is to visit one of the doctors to have the offending tooth removed. This particular hardship was forcefully brought home to me because Mrs Mokoena's few remaining teeth were a constant source of pain and trouble to her. On several occasions I accompanied her to the doctor. Once, when she was suffering more than usual, we arrived at one of the surgeries to be told that it was not a 'tooth-pulling' day as there were so many patients. I misguidedly suggested to the receptionist that Mrs Mokoena could have a more expensive private consultation with the doctor, only to be told that Blacks were only treated "around the back of the building at the clinic". We then went to one of the other clinics, where I was reprimanded once again, this time for accompanying Mrs Mokoena "around the back" of the surgery and not staying in the front where I belonged. However, despite the expense, these surgeries are always packed — mostly with Transkeians.

The hospital, which is under the control of the Natal Provincial Administration (NPA), is notable in that it lacks an out-patients department. According to one of the doctors, the reason for this is that such a service would be utilised exclusively by Blacks from Transkei, the cost of which would have to be borne by the NPA.

The local doctors do, however, refer Transkeian patients for in-patient treatment at the hospital. The hospital also accepts casualties who are brought for treatment, and every time I visited, the Black wards were always full, often with children sleeping two or three to a cot and sleeping on the floor. The Whites' section of the hospital, by contrast, was usually fairly empty.

Problems arise when patients are referred to the hospital by the clinic in Maluti, for Transkeians are supposed to be sent to the **Transkeian** hospital at Mount Fletcher which is situated about 64 kilometres from Maluti along very poor roads (see map 2). So, upon arrival at the hospital in Matatiele, there is a possibility that one can be turned away and told to go to Mount Fletcher. It is for this reason that personnel at the Maluti clinic tell people to go to town, but advise them not to mention that they have seen the doctor at the clinic, and to remove all bandages or plasters which might 'give away' their clinic consultation.

It could be argued that it is not unreasonable for an independent country to object to foreign nationals crossing their border in order to utilise their health-care facilities. However, as locals see it, Matatiele is their town. One Transkeian shopkeeper made the point that — "all shops from here (Transkei) and Lesotho buy from Matat. Why do we have to have a passport? Matat. is our town, we were born here . . . Matat. is our mother town which has grown us up". As discussed earlier, the town's commercial success requires the support of local Black people, so much so that it is obvious to even the casual traveller that it is Black business that has, and continues to 'grow Matatiele town up'. Understood in this context, the resentment that people express about being forced to deal with the Transkeian administration appears to be most reasonable. Why should a sick person, living in an area where there are poor roads and a limited transport system, be obliged to travel over 60 kilometres as opposed to 15 kilometres, to use what is believed by many to be inferior facilities, when prior to 1976 this problem did not arise?

This brings us to the question of whether or not the medical care that is available in Transkei is indeed inferior to that offered in South Africa. At the ceremonial opening of the Maluti Health Centre in February 1984, the audience was told that the clinic was one of the best in the country and that they were fortunate to be in Transkei where health services are better than in other developing countries. Why then, did the majority of St. Paul's villagers questioned, say that they preferred to spend R8 or more plus R1,20 return bus fare to consult the private doctors in town, when they could, for a fee of R1, see the doctor at the local clinic which is within walking distance and on the bus route (R1 return fare)? For those, who for a variety of possible reasons do not have a passport, there was, at the time no choice but to go to the clinic.

The clinic, although only 'officially' opened in 1984, started operating in 1981. It is a modern building fully equipped with a mini-operating theatre and small wards on one side of an open plan lecture area, and a reception desk, consulting rooms and dispensary on the other side. However, the theatre and wards are never used because of lack of funds and understaffing. Instead, the doctor and staff of seven nurses attend to minor ailments, 'maternities' and immunizations. Lectures (which at times resemble harangues) are given by the nursing staff each day whilst patients wait to see the doctor, and are on topics ranging from hygiene to tuberculosis to family planning. The doctor, who is in attendance in the mornings only, is a foreign national with no previous African experience, and is viewed with some suspicion as a result. This is just one of the instances of foreigners being recruited by the Transkeian government to work on a contract basis. Most of these people come from either Sri Lanka or Nigeria and work in the fields of education, medicine and engineering. According to a senior bureaucrat at Maluti, Sri Lankans and Nigerians are imported into the country at great expense because of a dearth of locally trained personnel and the failure of South Africans to apply for posts within Transkei.

The doctor at Maluti speaks neither Xhosa nor Sesotho and many people commented that the heavily accented English is also incomprehensible to them. Another cause for complaint was that the doctor rarely examines patients — just asks them a few questions via an interpreter and then writes out a prescription. The doctors in town also work with interpreters (with the exception of the Black doctor) but the difference seems to be that they have a far greater familiarity with, and understanding of, local health problems.

Unfortunately the aforementioned doctor has not, so far, been able to inspire many patients with confidence and this attitude is made worse by the fact that some of the nursing staff share the same view. The nurses often take it upon themselves to treat patients and administer drugs like antibiotics without referring to the doctor. I witnessed this at first-hand when my friends' children were diagnosed as having measles and then given penicillin injections and medicine to take home, all without reference to the doctor. Further problems at the clinic are caused by lack of drugs at the dispensary, which means that patients must either do without or else travel into town to purchase them from the private clinics or from the chemist.

Lack of transport also creates grave difficulties. Cases that the clinic cannot handle, including birth complications, must be referred to Mount Fletcher hospital. What does a very ill patient do in this situation?

A few weeks after my arrival in St. Paul's, I went to visit a woman who I had heard was very ill. When I arrived at the house it was to discover that all three of the occupants were incapacitated. The old woman was incapable of movement, delirious with fever and unable even to brush away the flies that were swarming around her face. She was left unattended by her daughter, who was herself ill with fever and vainly trying to soothe her baby who had diarrhoea. It was clear that the old woman was dying. To get a car owner in the village to make a special journey to the clinic or the hospital in town would cost R10 during the day, and R20 after 9 pm — money which this family certainly did not have. An ambulance from town could not come into Transkeian territory to pick up a patient and so I decided to go to the clinic and get them to send an ambulance to St. Paul's. However, at Maluti I was told that the clinic no longer had any transport and was not running the mobile clinics that had been in operation previously. This means that the only mobile clinic that serves the district is run on a private basis by the practice of four doctors from town (with consultations at R8 a time). The Combi from Maluti had been sent to Mount Fletcher to help their single ambulance.

The request for an ambulance was received with a certain amount of irritation, but eventually Mount Fletcher hospital was called by telephone and the ambulance summoned. "And what'll happen if there's an emergency delivery in the meantime and the ambulance is needed?" I was asked somewhat accusingly. Despite the pressure of this possible contingency, the ambulance driver, when he arrived, was quite happy to disappear to a nearby party for a drink. The invalids' family were left to load their relatives into the back of the 'ambulance' — a vehicle with two bench seats — and wait until the driver had finished. Upon his return, he unsuccessfully tried to extract a R2 'ambulance fee', changing his mind after being asked for a receipt. The patients did eventually get to Mount Fletcher hospital and all three recovered in time (the old woman spent over two months in hospital).

The point must be made that St. Paul's villagers and their neighbours are served by a modern clinic with a doctor and qualified nursing staff at comparatively low cost. The clinic is a centre for health education and a place from which staff can be sent out into the district on immunization programmes, etc. It sounds well and good on paper, but in reality people are faced with an inefficient and unsatisfactory system with which they are obliged to deal as a direct result of Transkeian 'independence'.

Conclusion

It has been my aim in this chapter to illustrate some of the less obvious ways that the new Transkeian administration in Matatiele impinges upon people's lives. For change is felt not only in the more predictable spheres of direct dealings with the bureaucracy, of which something has already been written (for example see James, 1983 and Maré, 1981 on difficulties with old age pensions). The on-going process of change that the transition to 'indpendence' has set in motion in Transkei, continues to bring frustrations and a miscellany of hardships to villagers many of which only become evident to the fieldworker after having lived there for a while.

As yet, there are no deeply entrenched divisions within St. Paul's, as very few villagers can be identified as beneficiaries of 'independence' in the way described by Southall and Charton. However, the temporary disruption caused by the soldiers on Donald's Farm and the feelings of animosity expressed for the wealthy member of the agricultural scheme, show the potential for such divisions to emerge. It is easy when speaking in broad economic terms, to say that Transkei is still part of the South African political and economic sphere. Nevertheless, 'independence' **has** had a significant impact on people's lives and as far as St. Paul's villagers are concerned, is certainly no fiction.

CHAPTER 3

LOCAL PERCEPTIONS OF GOVERNMENT — ISSUES OF BLACK AND WHITE

In the beginning, God asked the three groups — the **Maburu** *[Afrikaners], the English and the Africans — what they wanted. The* **Maburu** *said that they wanted land and to this day they are the best farmers in the country. The English asked for good brains and everyone knows that they are the cleverest people. Then God asked the Africans and they said— "oh we were just accompanying these others" and they didn't ask for anything. That is why the Blacks are in the position that they're in today (from a speech made at St. Paul's 'Farmer's Day').*

In Chapter Two my aim was to demonstrate that Transkeian 'independence' has had important consequences for ordinary St. Paul's villagers. In this chapter I wish to develop the theme of local perceptions of post-'independence' government, in particular, the commonly held belief that the shortcomings of the Transkeian government are attributable to the fact that it is Black. Whilst in St. Paul's, I was subjected to many a discussion by villagers on the incompetence of Blacks in the spheres of government, entrepreneurial skills and learning, and the inherent inferiority of Blacks to Whites. On pointing to the successes of the local store owner and people like him, I would be told that it was only because these people had White backing. These storekeepers are not the real owners, I was often told, they are just managers working for White bosses who live in Durban. The fact that White businessmen sometimes visited the local store provided incontrovertible 'proof' of this 'fact' as far as most villagers were concerned.

When I first arrived in Matatiele, I was inclined to believe that villagers merely told me these things because I am White and they thought that it was what I wanted to hear. Nevertheless, as the weeks went by and people became more and more frank with me, and after having long discussions on the topic with Mrs Mokoena, I began to realise that my informants were in earnest on this issue. However, it is not enough merely to record these kinds of beliefs, noting perhaps in passing that they are not true. It must be recognised first of all that these perceptions constitute reality for the people who hold them, and once this is understood, it is necessary to delve a little deeper in order to seek some explanations for their existence. "It would be simple" says Aron, "to distinguish, on the one hand, the real situation of the individual and, on the other, the idea which he has of it. But his idea of it is part of the reality one studies" (1969:67). It is the aim of this chapter to look critically at this "reality" and in so doing to suggest ways for its interpretation.

The 'Good Old Days' of White Rule

One of the major reasons for the high regard accorded to Whites, was that villagers looked back with nostalgia on the days when Matatiele was still 'under' South Africa and compared the contemporary situation with the 'good old days'. The changes that are associated with the coming of 'independence' are also associated with the passing of the Whites. Apart from the fact that the past often does look better from the vantage point of the present, people have very real reasons for believing that their standard of living has declined in the years since 'independence'. As I outlined in Chapter Two, there **are** high levels of corruption and inefficiency in the current administration and, in addition, the period since 1976 has seen a steady increase in unemployment and inflation rates. The blame for all of these things is placed at the door of the Matanzima government and is regarded as proof of the inability of Blacks to 'rule' themselves. It made no difference when I pointed out to villagers that the whole of South Africa is suffering from economic malaise and that unemployment and rising consumer costs cannot be blamed on the Transkeian government — people simply retorted that things were better when the Whites were in charge.

Increased taxation since 'independence' is a particularly sore point and is something that is felt very keenly by almost everybody. The fact that widows now have to pay a hut tax of R20 per annum along with men, was one of the most often mentioned causes for complaint. Furthermore, each household in Transkei is now obliged to pay a R60 levy, spread over three years, to pay for government tractors that were imported from Austria. People felt that it was adding insult to injury when it was announced on the radio that these tractors were being sold to the public whilst Transkeians were still contributing to their purchase cost. Mr Motebele, a man who had been forced to give up work in Johannesburg as a result of ill-health and who was unemployed at the time of our conversation, explained the situation as follows —

> We were happy to hear that we were going to get independence, but now that we've got it we are suffering a lot — we were better under the Whites. The first reason is tax. An adult under the Whites had a site and field and was paying hut tax of R5 and the youths were paying R2,50. Now it's very difficult because the adults have to pay R20 and the youths R10. Most of the people during the time of the Whites had fields, but now with this government most of the people have no fields. Since the homelands were made, prices have gone up all over the country and we are aware that it is because of these independences. Surely everything has changed nowadays. For wealthy people it's nice especially when it comes to the agricultural scheme. We poor people cannot afford to pay high prices. Wealthy people appreciate it. The wealthy people are the shopkeepers and those who have butcheries.

Here we can see very clearly the way in which all current misfortunes are lumped together and placed at the door of the Transkeian authorities. There is little recognition of the fact that growing population pressures in Transkei have meant that fewer and fewer people have rights to land and that the responsibility for this can, more properly, be attributed to the South African government's policy of separate development, which **obliges** Blacks to live in overcrowded 'homelands' in the first place.

My respondents in St. Paul's were not fully conscious of these aspects of their situation. This is borne out by people saying that they have never really suffered from apartheid in Matatiele and that apartheid is something which 'happens' in towns. There was even a great deal of confusion about what apartheid is, for, as more than one informant stated — "it is very hard to know whether there is less or more apartheid now when we are not really sure what it is to start off with". Another commented that there is no apartheid in Matatiele, with the exception of nearby Matatiele town where — "there is only a little bit here and there and we don't mind because we have grown up with it". But while many villagers are not sure about apartheid, do not question that they are living in a 'homeland', and must carry passes [at the time of writing] and are confused and puzzled over news of unrest in the urban areas, they **are** sure that they are oppressed and that life, for them, is a struggle for survival. As mentioned in Chapter Two, there is a general recognition that there are more expenses to be met in recent years. In addition to the taxes that must be paid, villagers are always being asked for compulsory contributions to various funds, said one exasperated woman —

> *we have to pay R60 for the tractors — we were worried if we don't pay they're going to take our cattle away. These seniors are killing us — whatever they say the people say 'yes'. The problem is that they start to ask the men things — if they discussed things with women it would be different. I am a widow — I paid R5 for this school [the local primary school], now I've got to pay R5 for the school at Ramohlakoana. This is forced, there's nothing I can do about it.*

Such observations were often couched in terms such that Whites were characterised as being good and Blacks as being incompetent and bad. Mrs Ramoshebe, a widow who makes ends meet by selling home-brewed beer, had this to say on the subject —

> *We are struggling nowadays — we weren't struggling like this before — now we build our own schools and dipping tanks — before the **makgoa** [White, plural — lekgoa] government was building them for us. This independence has brought us to burn — we widows work as men — nobody is looking after us. Before when lekgoa were here people were charged for **diretlo** [ritual murders] now they just get let out of prison after a few months, they know how to make **tjhotjho** [bribes].*

Her neighbour added to this list of woes the fact that —

> *When the **lekgoa** were near us here on the farms we got mealies and sheep cheaply. Even now the **lekgoa** farmers sell more cheaply — but now they are far away, also they gave us piece jobs. Since the **lekgoa** left the place the Blacks sell things at very high prices, not like they do in town.*

As mentioned earlier, many Transkeians commute into Matatiele town daily and make wide use of the shopping and medical facilities available to them there. Most interviewees regretted that the time had passed when they could utilise all the facilities in the town, like the magistrate's offices and the police station. They spoke of pre-'independence' days as a period of justice, fair play and harmony and of Whites as people who display qualities of generosity, mercy and kindness. Even the presence of the SAP roadblock is blamed on the Transkeian government, rather than on the South Africans. As one old man put it — "with the South Africans we were not required to carry so many passes (sic) which are useless. Now we have to have a passport, book of life and a **dompas** and they all cost money".

Matatiele Town — its Place in the District

Prior to 1976, Kaiser Matanzima repeatedly demanded the inclusion of the East Griqualand region (of which Matatiele town is a part) into Transkei as a condition of his accepting 'independence'. This request was made on the grounds that the area was historically Xhosa territory and so should be part of the Xhosa 'national state'. As it happened, Matanzima finally did accept 'independence' without this condition being met, but this meant that the East Griqualand area, which was part of the Cape Province, was now cut off from the rest of the Cape by the intervening 'independent' Transkeian territory (see map 1). The South African government commissioned an official inquiry into the status of East Griqualand and on the basis of the report it was decided, in 1978, to include the region into Natal. This measure was the ostensible reason for Matanzima's decision to break off diplomatic ties with the only country with which Transkei had diplomatic relations, that is, South Africa (cf. Streek and Wicksteed, 1981:171-9; Southall, 1983:268-71). Diplomatic relations were re-established in 1980 and East Griqualand (save for some farm land which was granted to Transkei) remained within Natal. However, the local issue of Matatiele town being incorporated into Transkei has not died out completely. In 1982, I attended a political rally in the district at which Prime Minister George Matanzima was most strident in his demands for the town (Segar, 1982). During my stay in the district, certain bureaucrats and businessmen were still talking about Transkei's legitimate claims to Matatiele town. Some of those in high office even disdainfully discussed the **improbability** of turning Maluti into a viable competitor for Matatiele town even though this now seems to be the official line. At all TNIP meetings and rallies, the leaders cry out "one nation!" to which those assembled must reply "one Transkei!". To this a local touch has been added by TNIP officials with the call "one Maluti!" to which the response is "one Matatiele!".

The views of St. Paul's villagers, however, were quite different, as most were vehemently opposed to the idea of Matatiele town becoming part of Transkei. If this happened, they argued, all the Whites would leave and the wholesalers, shops and hospital would all collapse much to the detriment of Transkeians. In the words of one local — "what would happen to all the supermarkets that are benefiting us there in Matat? They would go away and we would be struggling. White people wouldn't want to stay there under Transkei". When the wife of a local politician proclaimed at a TNIP meeting that, "we are still weeping for our town Matatiele" she was greeted with gales of laughter. Others suggested that Matatiele district **should** be reunited with its town, but that this should be achieved by the district moving into Natal rather than the other way around.

Exploring Some Explanations

At this point we must stop and ask ourselves **why** it should be that Matatiele villagers have internalised such feelings of inferiority about themselves, and how has it come about that White South Africans are characterised as the 'good guys'. Furthermore, we need to examine more fully people's equation of all that is bad, like unemployment and inflation, with the Matanzima government rather than with the South African government.

1)   The Unpopularity of the Transkeian Government

As I have tried to show so far, villagers do have good reason to complain about their government as it is represented at the local level. For it is true that people have to bribe some government officials in order to obtain such things as pensions, passports, places in high school for their children and favourable judgments in the settlement of disputes. And even the payment of bribes does not necessarily guarantee results; many people have waited, and continue to wait for years, before receiving their state pensions. Of **61** St. Paul's villagers who were of pensionable age, **28 (45,9%)** were receiving government pensions and an additional **7 (11,5%)** received pensions from past employers, the remaining **26 (42,6%)** received no pensions although they were eligible for them. In a community where cash is a scarce and much needed resource, a state pension (R96 every second month for women over 60 and men over 65) often means the difference between survival and slow starvation.

The problems that abound in the local government schools are also very distressing. Teachers are often to be found in drinking places rather than in the classroom, and it was not uncommon for Mrs Mokoena and myself to come across whole classes of pupils who had been sent by their teacher upon some small errand to the shop during school hours. At a TNIP meeting where general grievances were being aired, someone from a nearby village told the assembly —

> *we have got a problem at our place, the school principal is always drunk and the other teacher has got his business — he is always in town and we have reported that to the inspector — but because they are bribing no further steps are taken. We are unhappy! We have tried to report this to Mr M [a local politician] to come and solve the problem. He did not come.*

It is also true that people with rank and office practise nepotism and enjoy exercising privilege and power to the detriment of 'ordinary' people. All of these things would naturally lead to resentment and bitterness being directed towards any government of the day. These problems are also by no means exclusive to Transkei. James (1983) and Maré (1981) discuss at length the issue of pensions in the 'homelands', and in particular in resettlement areas. They describe how people have to wait years before receiving their pensions and have difficulties in applying for them in the first place because they often do not have birth certificates and so cannot prove their age. An important contributory factor to these problems, they suggest, is the confusion that stems from the decentralisation occurring when 'homeland' governments accede to power —

> *At a certain point, the responsibility for administering pensions was transferred from central government to the homeland authorities, which burdened these authorities with an impossibly large workload. This load was augmented by the sudden sharp increases in population in homeland resettlement areas . . . (James, 1983:31).*

This sudden administrative overload must occur in many government departments and should be understood as one of the factors contributing to bureaucratic inefficiency, which in its turn contributes to Transkeians' disillusionment with their government.

It must not be forgotten either, that the TNIP can hardly be justified in their claim of a popular mandate to rule Transkei. "There has never been such a thing as a free vote for the mass of the voters in Transkei" say Streek and Wicksteed (1981:25), and Southall (1983:120) is equally forceful, commenting that "bantustan elections have been far from free, and within Transkei the electoral system utilized in the four pre-independence elections was designed and operated so as to deliberately distort popular opinion . . .". He goes on to identify the ways in which these distortions came about as — "the utilization of chiefs and headmen as agents of electoral control; secondly, the restriction of electoral activity by candidates and persons opposed to the policies of separate development; and thirdly, the limitation of urban influence in the electoral process". Laurence (1976:85-89) also elaborates on the same themes and points out that as over half of the Transkeian population is illiterate, people required assistance when casting their votes. The names of candidates were read out to voters who then communicated their choices verbally to the polling officer who completed the actual ballot paper. "Whatever the justification for the procedure, it cannot be described as a secret vote. By any logical definition, a secret vote is known only to the person making it" (Laurence, 1976:88).

The interviews that I had with St. Paul's villagers corroborate these views. The first Transkeian elections were held in 1963 when the region was granted self-government. One woman recalled the voting procedure as follows —

> *When we were still living at Ramohlakoana, we were called to the Tribal Authority [at Ramohlakoana] to have our* **dompasses** *stamped [to be registered as a voter]. We were told by the headmen that when we got there we would be helped by the teachers we found there. We were given a piece of paper with 25 names on and we had to choose two. The teachers were to help those who couldn't read or write — they held the hand and ticked for the person — so the teachers just ticked the ones they liked — it was cheating.*

Speaking of the 1976 elections another woman told me —

> *I voted for the man who hired trucks to take the people to the Tribal Authority. He said he was going to speak for us at the parliament.*

Someone else said that he just voted for two names that he recognised, but did not know what it was for. The chief had told the villagers that if they did not go to have their passes stamped and cast their vote they would all be sent to live in Qwa Qwa (the official South Sotho 'homeland').

In order to understand the particular powerlessness of Transkeian villagers, it is worthwhile to consider and compare briefly the responses of Tanzanian peasants to an independent government. According to Hyden (1980), African countries south of the Sahara with the exceptions of South Africa and Zimbabwe, have economies based on small scale rural production and as such, a great deal of political leverage rests in the countryside with the people who have control over their own means of subsistence. He suggests that in Tanzania the relative autonomy that rural smallholders have by virtue of their economic independence, places them, to a certain extent, outside the power of the ruling classes and in a favourable bargaining position. When this is the case, the trump card that small peasant producers hold, is their ability to withdraw support for the government —

> *In Africa the course of events is determined as much by those with power to withdraw from state policies as it is by those who actually make and execute these policies. Peasants can often trade the threat of withdrawal of support for the regime for resources the state commands (Hyden, 1980:33).*

Hyden argues that the Tanzanian peasantry are in a sense "uncaptured" by the state by virtue of their self-sufficiency; and it is their peripheral, "uncaptured" position which gives them a relatively powerful voice. In contrast, Transkeian villagers are in a situation of powerlessness and economic dependence and they characterise themselves as victims, helpless and frustrated in the face of a government which only takes from them, giving nothing in return. They present no threat to the Transkeian authorities, who can thus afford to ignore them with impunity. The current situation has to be seen in the context of the demise of an independent and thriving peasant agriculture in South Africa. This process of African under-development, resulted from a battery of discriminatory legislation, such as the Land Acts of 1913 and 1936, and is described in detail by Wilson (1971), Bundy (1972; 1979), Molteno (1977), Murray — the Lesotho case — (1981) and others. They describe how peasant self-sufficiency was steadily undermined by White capital-ists who needed cheap labour both for the industrial and mining sector and for farming — "In broad terms, the decade after the [Anglo-Boer war] was one in which a sustained, several-pronged offensive was launched by white legislators and administrators . . . against the self-reliance and independence of the peasantry" (Bundy, 1972:383). The long-term effects of such legislation have resulted in the over-population of the 'homeland' areas from which people are obliged to migrate in search of employment. Those left behind enjoy neither economic self-suffi-ciency, nor political leverage, and this latter point is illustrated most forcefully by accounts of TNIP meetings in St. Paul's.

The local branch of the TNIP had kept minutes of its meetings since 1979, to which I was given access. These documents are chronicles of the everyday frustrations experienced by the villagers. The meetings very often centred around the topic of getting the senior TNIP members to come and listen to their grievances and convey them to the government in Umtata. The problems most often cited were lack of pensions, the inadequacies of the local dipping tank and water tank, the need for more residential sites and better school facilities. Usually, meetings were devoted to discussing the preparations for forthcoming meetings which party officials were going to attend. These visits entailed collecting money for refresh-ments and gifts, and putting on entertainments for the visitors who were to come to listen to complaints and problems and "take them to the parliament". It appeared from the minutes, that it was not uncommon for officials simply not to turn up at these meetings, for which elaborate preparations had sometimes been made as this extract illustrates —

[We were] waiting for the visitors to come and solve our problems. The chairman went to the bus stop early in the morning to see those coming from the different places. At 7am he was already standing there. He waited there with the school, waiting as they had prepared so many plays to meet the visitors with. Now they are standing there until very late, waiting. The time now is 12 o' clock — still waiting. The chairman is going to town to see what has happened. [Upon his return with the news that the visitors are not coming] The people came in the house and prayed . . . then the chairman asked them — "what can be done about all these expenses?" Mr N said, "expenses are nothing, what we want is for these people to come".

Other meetings concentrated on how the TNIP was to increase its small membership (and even smaller participation of members) in the village. Often members would ask each other what TNIP is, and the confusion that this question caused in the minds of many is reflected in the following minuted exchange —

> *Mrs F said they should explain about the TNIP. Mrs M explained that TNIP is for the government — it should be respected. Mr T said TNIP is love. TNIP is going to solve our problems. TNIP says you should love your neighbours. Mr S agreed and said TNIP is a preacher all over the country. Mr L asked if there was any paper from the government of constitution which gives the instructions. Mr S said they had got no instructions . . . the chairman said that we need instructions for the TNIP.*

Approximately 112 St. Paul's villagers belonged to TNIP and of these only about 20-40 regularly attended the monthly party meetings. In other words, only 11% of the de facto village population were TNIP members and a mere 2%-4% attended meetings. Usually the same people were present at meetings and these tended to be the same individuals who attended **dipitso**, and who were members of the school committee and of various church committees. Many of the 'regulars' were on the TNIP committee (which usually comprised ten people), and office holders (i.e. chair and deputy, secretary and treasurer) were given bus fare in order to attend district and regional meetings. However, what little prestige that could be gained by being a TNIP committee member, was diminished by the fact that hardly anybody wanted to join the party or attend the meetings. Members were usually recruited through a network of family and friends. For example, Mr Mokoena and other members of the Mokoena family, joined because Mr Mokoena's aunt was a TNIP committee member. Mr Mokoena told me that he had given his aunt the 50c membership fee in order to make her happy, but that he was not interested in attending any meetings.

This edited version of a local TNIP meeting (taken from the minute book) is a typical example of the discussion at one of these gatherings and illustrates the perennial concern over lack of members and lack of enthusiasm for the party.

Translated (by Mrs Mokoena) from the TNIP minutes . . .

The meeting was at St. Paul's, it was opened by the prayer of Mr S. The secretary read the minutes of the last meeting. The chairman asked if they were right. Mr L said, "no, I am complaining. My name has not appeared there — why? I was the first to stand and speak. Always when I stand you mock at me because nobody likes me." The secretary apologised . . . Mr M said "This TNIP should be preached to people who do not know it". Mr L put a sum of R1,40 on the table and said that the money was for Father P and his wife. "They have joined the TNIP although the priest has got no time to come." Mrs N said "the law is that the one who wants to join should come personally, we should not make people join on the streets, they should come to the meeting and join." . . .

Mrs J said "Let us be strong — the TNIP is the future of our children — others joined in 1978, until now I've never seen them — they don't come to the TNIP — can we call them TNIP members?" Mrs N agreed, she said — "TNIP is not playing — can't you see we read the minutes every time and we write down these 50c [membership dues] every time. Let's go forward it's very good to be TNIP members.". . .

Mr L stood up and said "People should join TNIP — everyone should have a card and a receipt. They like to spend their money where it's not necessary, but here at TNIP it's necessary that one should have a new card. How are they going to be called TNIP members?" Mrs B agreed, "everyone should support the government" she said. Mr L said "to make people attend meetings, they should be marked absent if they don't come. People are not paying taxes, when they've got problems they want people who are paying taxes to stand for them. They should send money if they are in the cities". The chairman said, "no — this is not tax — one should come and pay in person, we don't want a big amount of money — but we want a big number of people". Mr L replied "those who are owing — are they still TNIP members? Those who have joined should attend the meetings". The chairman said "Let's not press them hard, let's preach to them until they understand, they should be encouraged to renew their cards for 50c." . . .

Mrs C said "It's late, let the next TNIP meeting be on the 11th. Let us close please." Mr S closed with a prayer.

Both members and non-members alike expressed scepticism about TNIP, whose purpose, most believed, was to solve people's problems, and this, they clearly saw was exactly what it was not doing. Rather than seeing themselves in a position of bargaining power, they regarded themselves as being at the mercy of the government and its officials. One woman summed this up by saying — "these seniors of TNIP have no love or mercy for people at all — if they had, it would work . . . TNIP is supposed to work for everyone, not just the friends and relatives of the seniors".

2)   The Image of the Benevolent White

In comparison with the contemporary situation, villagers feel strongly that their past life 'under the Whites' was far preferable. They pointed out that in the past, maintenance of facilities like dipping tanks and schools was far more efficient, and that White officials were more impartial in the settling of disputes and in the dispensation of justice. Gluckman (1968) sought to explain the good relationship that often pertained between White commissioners and rural people in Zululand and Northern Rhodesia. The argument that he puts forward is, I believe, equally pertinent in explaining the nostalgia expressed by Transkeian villagers when speaking of pre-'independence' days. Gluckman notes first of all that commissioners were usually men who had received a professional training, and as a consequence espoused a certain professional ethic which committed them to service and development of the community in which they were to work. He argues that in pursuance of this objective many 'native commissioners' endeavoured to establish and maintain good personal relationships with the people and to work as far as possible in their interests. Gluckman saw the commissioners as occupying a special niche in the government hierarchy which enabled them to gain the trust and respect of the people amongst whom they worked. This he refers to as their **inter-hierarchical role**. Writing specifically about Zululand, Gluckman reminds us that at this time chiefs, who had had their powers severely restricted, were now working in a role that was supposed to be supportive of the government. They therefore found themselves to be the butt of much resentment and suspicion, whereas the commissioner who was not considered as having any necessary moral commitment to the people and who now wielded more power than the chiefs, was seen as a means of achieving both protection and assistance from the higher authorities (1968:80). In addition, one should note that commissioners, unlike chiefs, had no local kinship ties amongst the people they were administering, a fact which probably contributed to their image of fair-mindedness.

Those commissioners who did see their duty to be one of helping and 'developing' the people, found they were sometimes at loggerheads with the central government. "It seemed to me" comments Gluckman, "that the standards set up were such that in South Africa the commissioners were more liberal to Africans than the Parliament in Cape Town they 'represented'" (1968:84). Thus their inter-hierarchical role gave commissioners certain advantages. Unlike the chiefs, they had power and connections and so were appreciated for their potentially useful role, and although these men were White, they were often judged on their individual merit and not necessarily as government representatives. Some commissioners were able to exercise a fair amount of initiative in the dispensation of their duties by simple virtue of the fact that they were situated so far away from the major centres where no one really saw or cared about what they were doing. Nevertheless, as Gluckman rightly points out, the commissioner was restricted by government policy and lack of funds to carry out any truly significant development. However "in local activity his actions, activities and attitudes contributed to a certain solidarity between Zulu and administration . . . this inter-hierarchical role of the commissioners contributed substantially both to the cohesion of the tribal area and even to establishing a certain consensus over values and loyalties across the color bar" (1968:79).

Positive feelings of solidarity and loyalty towards **local** government officials in Matatiele have remained and, coloured by the passage of time and comparison with the present unsatisfactory state of affairs, have possibly grown even stronger. These sentiments (not surprisingly) are also shared by some of the White townspeople. For example, one man whose family had owned a trading station in the district, recalled how the villagers often discussed their problems with their local shopkeepers. As the White community was so small, the shopkeeper invariably knew the magistrate and the police commissioner and other prominent bureaucrats, and so could often solve an individual's problems simply by making a telephone call. "We were good to them, and they knew it," said one ex-trader, "of course they'd like to have us back there, now they're suffering at the hands of their own people, it's a tragedy".

Why is it then, that local Transkeian officials have not taken over the inter-hierarchical role described by Gluckman and sought to work for the interests of the people in their local area? Gluckman himself suggests that in newly independent African states, the professional ethic of the old style White commissioners, used to working in relative isolation, is replaced by the party ethic of enthusiastic party representatives keen to ensure some form of consistency in the new administration of the country (1968:85). Officials therefore are less concerned with local level interests and a period of dissatisfaction and disorganisation may result.

Less speculative and hypothetical is Hyden's analysis of the bureaucracy in post-independence Tanzania. He describes a situation where the new bureaucracy had very little to offer a largely self-supporting peasantry. The social amenities that people desired had already been promised free of charge by the government, and so the bureaucracy could provide few incentives for co-operation in the government's scheme of increased agricultural production (part of the local socialist policy known as **ujamaa**). He notes that the bureaucracy comprised of people whose careers were primarily concerned with the administration of party policies, and that first and foremost their loyalty lay with the party (TANU) and the president. Their jobs, then, depended upon their success in being able to implement the **ujamaa** policy. "In this situation," says Hyden, "it is not surprising that the bureaucrats, virtually without exception, turned to an authoritarian, managerial approach" (1980:106).

Villagers in Matatiele also experience their local bureaucracy as one which is "authoritarian" and "managerial". However, the bureaucrats' approach, in this instance, cannot be explained in terms of either excessive revolutionary zeal or frustration at not being able to implement policy. Rather, they comprise a group of people whose primary concern is their own aggrandizement and accumulation of wealth; this is not to suggest that these motives cannot be attributed to similar groups in other countries, but I would suggest that in this instance these motives are the only ones of any significance. It is also true (cf. Chapter Two above) that their loyalties lie with the ruling party, TNIP, which has, since 1976, provided opportunities and good salaries to an increasingly large civil service. The Transkeian administrator, working in a rural area like Matatiele, is not an outsider in the same way that the 'native commissioner' was. Usually these bureaucrats have grown up in rural villages, but later their aim is to dissociate themselves as much as possible from the majority of Transkeians who are poor and unsophisticated.

There is no 'inter-hierarchical role' for the local bureaucrat, whose 'ethic' is that of the promotion of his/her own welfare, and whose identification of interests lies with the party rather than with the people. Furthermore, the Transkeian administrator comes to the job not as a result of some popular revolution, but as a result of the South African government's 'homeland' policy. As Southall puts it (1983:176) —

> *The essence of the bantustan programme in the Transkei was the superimposition upon the reserve economy of the apparatus of an Africanized state. Accordingly, as Pretoria progressively devolved functions upon Umtata, so was there need for marked expansion of the local administration; and a key feature of the project, of course, was that the new bureaux should become staffed by Transkeian bureaucrats whose material interests would lead them to identify with the autonomous existence of a Xhosa polity.*

3)   Images of Self

So far I have been discussing various reasons as to why villagers believe that living under a Transkeian government is worse than being directly subject to the White South African administration. However, the points raised do not necessarily explain why villagers in St. Paul's have such a low self-image, why their dissatisfaction with the government is so often couched in racial terms ("we **Blacks** can't govern ourselves") and why Whites are characterised in the following ways —

> *I liked the Whites because they were feeling for us — they were kind. All of these things that I have been telling you about didn't happen when we were under the Whites.*

> *Things were far better under the Whites. Most of us like the Whites because we are pulling hard since they have left. For every group of Blacks — once they get a high rank — they just think of their families and not of poor people. Whites are nice and they are clever, they are not selfish when they get a high place in the office.*

> *I grew up with these Whites in Matat. and know them very much, I also know these Blacks and I would prefer it if these Whites stayed here and it remained South Africa.*

> *A calf feeds from its own mother and how would it be if you took the mother away? That's how it is if you take the Whites away from us — we have fed from their breasts.*

In order to come to grips with this problem, it is necessary to take cognisance of the historical experience of colonised peoples This experience has inculcated into both colonised and colonisers the sense of White superiority and the desirability of the European lifestyle. A dominant group will thrust its values onto its subjects, and when the subjects themselves begin to believe in these values, then the domination is complete. As Davidson (1961:25) puts it, "[T]o be treated as an inferior is often to become an inferior . . .". This situation comes about where one group of people dominates another, and in the context of colonial Africa, where the dominant groups have been White and the dominated Black, the relationship has the added dimension of always being articulated in terms of race.

In Chapter One, I discussed the way in which advertisers promote various consumer products and in so doing, establish and foster new **needs** amongst people. Lappé and Collins 1980) discuss the crude advertising and marketing campaigns that multinational companies employ in their efforts to gain footholds in Third World markets. Advertising ploys that the parent companies would be prosecuted for in Europe and the United States, their subsidiaries successfully get away with in the 'developing countries'. Most of the thrust, they explain, is directed at building up the status of consumer goods against more traditional diets. The result is that people end up spending more money and receiving less nutrition, a grave problem in rural areas where infant mortality and malnutrition-related disease rates increase each year.

> *With this advertising effort, even those with very little money are reached. It persuades them that food in a package has special powers. Its subtle message is that their traditional diets of beans, corn, millet and rice are worthless compared to what westerners eat (Moore Lappé and Collins, 1982:237).*

Hall (1974:9-34) traces the pressures — technological, economic and commercial — that have led to "lifeless" white bread becoming fashionable and increasingly lacking in nutritional goodness. He notes that the colour white has come to be associated with certain qualities like goodness, purity and high birth, and white flour in its turn has become linked with high standards of living, refinement and snob-appeal. These feelings usually result in the rich being "the first to adopt the fruits of the latest technology, leading the way to eventual adoption by the general public" (Hall, 1974:14). This is an interesting reflection on what is happening in St. Paul's and other villages like it, where people are caught up in an escalating spiral of 'keeping up with the Jones's' with all the expense (and often nutritional loss that this entails. It also forms part of the wider syndrome of regarding the lifestyle of the Whites as being superior and something to aspire to.

Hall emphasises the fact that ". . . the value of an article of food is determined not by the content of protein, carbohydrates, etc., but by its symbolic value — as it appeals to the appetite, the emotions, the soul" (1974:45). In the same way White colonisers in Africa (and elsewhere) projected their values onto the indigenous population, asserting the merits of their lifestyles, morals and 'whiteness'. By natural implication, then, the lifestyles, morals and 'blackness' of the colonised were seen as being undesirable and inferior, values which should be abandoned in favour of those of the colonisers.

Ranger (1983) relates how colonisers in Africa, particularly the British, were at pains to stress to Africans the values of their own European traditions. He points out that these traditions were upheld and practised in Africa by the colonials with far more vigour and attention to detail than they ever were in the mother country. He calls this the invention of tradition, and makes special reference to institutions like the army and schools where Africans were trained to value, to an exaggerated degree, 'qualities' of discipline, loyalty to the school or the regiment and respect for school and regimental traditions. In particular, the concept of hierarchy was always stressed, be it on the parade ground, in the classroom or in the offices of the local administration. Africans were taught that in order to become successful they had to model themselves on their European colonisers and the European-invented traditions that were upheld as paradigms for their behaviour. Needless to say, Blacks were trained to accept positions at the **bottom** of European hierarchies, as Ranger (1983:227) phrases it —

> *European invented traditions offered Africans a series of clearly defined points of entry into the colonial world, though in almost all cases it was entry into the subordinate part of a man/master relationship. They began by socializing Africans into acceptance of one or other readily available European neo-traditional modes of conduct — the historical literature is full of Africans proud of having mastered the business of being a member of a regiment or having learnt how to be an effective practitioner of nineteenth-century Anglicanism.*

Part of this process of domination entails the destruction of respect, amongst the subordinate group themselves, for their own lifestyle and values. It is not surprising then, that Blacks should endeavour to 'imitate' European 'civilisation' and to see in it a means of self-improvement. For the acquisition of a European lifestyle — education, job and the material trappings that go with it — enabled Blacks to escape from the 'uncivilised' life which they had consistently been taught to despise.

Magubane (1971) grapples with this problem of Blacks' low self-appraisal. He acknowledges its existence as having resulted from domination, but suggests that this internalisation of feelings of inferiority is somehow not real. For he says (1971:428) that —

> *It is evident that as long as a group is dominated by another, it "accepts" and "lives" the role imposed on it as a matter of course. . . . The colonial situation was that of forced subordination; we must judge in the light of this reality the values and images to which Africans "aspired" before we accept them as genuine.*

He suggests that Blacks under colonialism who attached prestige to such things as a light skin or European clothing, were in a "warped psychological state" and suffering from a form of "mass insanity". He argues, therefore, that Blacks never actually internalised these values but merely enacted them —

> *... urban Africans could not internalize the industrial culture; they were*
> *merely uprooted and divorced from the enrichment of their own culture,*
> *without receiving any substitute other than objects; they were sounding*
> *brass and tinkling cymbals, being without love, being true to nothing*
> *(1971:430).*

In a reply to this particular point, Epstein maintains that what is being described is "the phenomenon of what is commonly called negative identity — a process whereby members of a subordinate group come to evaluate their own behaviour in terms of the norms and values of the dominant group" (1971:432). I believe that this is a more adequate explanation of St.Paul's villagers' feelings of inferiority. It would explain also why these feelings still persist after the departure of Whites, and how elite groups of Blacks are able to take over the role of the dominant group and maintain the same values of superiority as did their predecessors. An elite, according to Cohen's (1981:xvi) definition, is "a collectivity of persons who occupy commanding positions in some important sphere of social life, and who share a variety of interests arising from similarities of training, experience, public duties, and way of life". What becomes clear, then, is that the elite group does not necessarily have to be White, but does necessarily have to share the same values and interests. This may seem fairly obvious, but I think that in a South African context where social life continues to be defined in terms of race, this point needs to be emphasised.

It is not surprising then, that in Matatiele an elite group of bureaucrats, entrepreneurs and professionals should seek to differentiate themselves as being superior in much the same terms as did their White predecessors. These people do not share with the villagers an attitude of low self-appraisal, but do not scruple at encouraging others to pay them the deference and respect that they have seen given to Whites. Those Blacks with position and wealth are known locally as 'lekgoa' (Whites), 'high ranks' or 'seniors' and are accorded preferential treatment; at all public functions such people sit separately from the 'common herd' and are given special foods. There is also a strong trend for differentiating at private parties and feasts between 'high ranking' special guests who eat 'Western style' at a table with plates, knives and forks and are given special fare, and 'common' people who sit on the floor and eat from communal dishes 'traditional style'. Those who enjoy a position amongst the 'seniors' are naturally happy to reinforce attitudes about their own superiority. They speak of themselves as being 'progressive' and 'civilised' and wish to dissociate themselves from ordinary villagers and their 'backward' ways.

The literature and the ethnography that I have presented in this chapter bring to mind the concept of 'false consciousness'. In the case of St. Paul's, we may say that the villagers who continue to believe in their own inferiority in relation to the 'lekgoa' — both White and Black — have a false consciousness. What is generally understood by false consciousness, in the Marxian sense, is that the true mechanisms of the exploitation of one class by another are obscured. The dominant class projects a certain world view, belief in which facilitates the domination of the subordinate class —

> *The ideas of the ruling class are in every epoch the ruling ideas, i.e. the class which is the ruling **material** force of society, is at the same time its ruling **intellectual** force. . . . The ruling ideas are nothing more than the ideal expression of the dominant material relationships, the dominant material relationships grasped as ideas; hence of the relationships which make the one class the ruling one, therefore, the ideas of its dominance (Marx and Engels, [1845-6] 1970:64).*

These ideas, as I have tried to show, often consist in believing in the truth and superiority of a group's world view, thus justifying and maintaining a particular set of social relations which work to the advantage of the dominant group. On the other side of the coin, false consciousness conceals from the subordinate group the true nature of their domination (cf. Goldberg, 1985). However, as Ryan (1985:125) succinctly puts it — "false consciousness is not a consciousness of falsehoods, but a systematically self-deceiving state of mind". He argues that Marx was not suggesting that people go around knowingly trying to deceive others, but that usually these beliefs are held sincerely. For example, capitalist employers usually believe that they are entering into voluntary relationships with workers, that these workers share with themselves identical civil rights and that therefore no injustices are being perpetrated against them (Ryan, 1985:126). Similarly, most European colonists were probably sincere in their beliefs that they were bringing a superior and uplifting way of life to Africa. And likewise, their Black subjects were proud and gratified when they achieved any advancement within the colonial hierarchy.

It follows then, that St. Paul's villagers are also being sincere in their continued belief in the illusion of their own inferiority.

Villagers' false consciousness or self-deception has led them to place the blame for all that is bad in Transkei on the Transkeian government and on Blacks themselves. The falseness of the illusion is that it is the White South African government, in collaboration with an elite group of Black Transkeians, who are responsible for the situation in Transkei today. Instead, antagonism and contempt are turned in upon the people themselves, who are thus, unwittingly, helping to support the status quo.

An important part of this situation, is the fact that citizenship of the various South African 'homelands' is based on ethnic identity, a state of affairs that often leads to tension and outright hostility. I shall be considering villagers' perceptions of ethnicity in the next two chapters, and Chapter Five, in particular, examines the issue of the revival of certain customs. This revivalism, and the emphasis that people place on the importance of 'tradition', must be seen along with the attitudes that have been described in this chapter. I do not believe that they are necessarily contradictory, but rather that these perceptions reflect the complexity of the reality of life for Transkeian villagers.

CHAPTER 4

THE IMPORTANCE OF ETHNIC IDENTITY

My aim in this chapter is to show how perceptions of ethnicity have to be studied in their particular political context, and how that context itself helps to define and shape perceived differences in ethnic identity. An issue that I shall be focussing upon is the way that notions of ethnicity are used by villagers as explanatory devices in the face of government inadequacies. People in St. Paul's were frequently ready to attribute local administrative inefficiency and corruption to ethnic animosities on the part of those in power, saying that in a Xhosa 'homeland' Basotho were treated like second class citizens. By the same token, those in authority used ethnic stereotypes to rebuff allegations of prejudice — according to them — Basotho were stupid and ignorant and so made unfounded accusations. There were times when it appeared to me that Basotho allegations were justified, but on other occasions it was more reasonable to attribute behaviour not to ethnic prejudice, but rather to the more generalised exploitation of the poor by the rich and powerful. For the ethnic antagonism and polarisation did not take place so much between local villagers in St. Paul's, but was usually directed towards the local bureaucrats — the representatives of the **Xhosa** government.

In fact as the data below illustrate, villagers of different ethnic identities live together quite amicably, they co-operate with one another, they even marry one another and most of them are united in voicing their dissatisfaction with the government. I would argue, however, that the fact that Basotho villagers voice this resentment in terms of ethnicity, shows that ethnicity could in time become the pretext for tensions and conflict within the village itself. At present the economic gulf which separates the majority of villagers from the bureaucratic elite, irrespective of their ethnic identity, means that most villagers have more in common than they have dividing them.

The Political Nature of Ethnicity in Transkei

It needs to be stressed that in the particular context of a South African 'homeland', ethnicity has special significance in so far as one's 'homeland' membership is determined by 'ethnic' identity (cf. Rogers, 1980:chapter 4). Consequently, people are inclined to be very conscious of their ethnicity. Furthermore, as Barth (1969:225) observed, an increase in ethnic consciousness commonly follows the passing of a colonial regime. In colonial situations, ethnic interactions were more likely to lead to the minimisation of cultural differences. For people's political relations and energies in these contexts are directed towards the over-arching administration. Removal of such a regime often has the opposite effect, as Barth puts it — the passing of a colonial government may lead to less "security" and a concomitant rise in "arbitrariness" and "violence" which in turn leads to less ethnic interaction and the promotion of ethnic boundaries.

Perhaps Horowitz's (1975) explanation of the increased awareness of ethnic identity in post-colonial countries is both more convincing and couched in more diplomatic language. He acknowledges that colonial rulers themselves both consciously and unconsciously promoted perceptions of ethnic differentiation. After all they identified themselves as (1975:131) "ethnically differentiated superiors" and encouraged their subjects to think in terms of rank and hierarchy. Horowitz (1975:130) goes on to say that —

> By channeling motivation and recruitment in preconceived directions, colonial policy gave the existence of the emerging groups a firmer basis in the groups' own perceptions than it might otherwise have had. The result was to make each group increasingly conscious of the aptitudes and disabilities, virtues and vices it supposedly held in common.

However, during colonial rule, ethnic conflict was not so common because the colony itself was a unit of identification towards which people directed their energies and antagonisms. But with the advent of independence, this unit of identification dwindled and the local context dramatically gained in significance. Nationalist movements had previously ignored ethnic differences whilst concentrating on the external force (colonial government), but were now left without a common rallying point and separate ethnic group identifications were free to proliferate. "Most members respond to downward shifts in significant political boundaries by downward shifts in the focus of group identity" (Horowitz, 1975:140; also cf. Manona, 1980:97-99).

Ranger (1983) also comments that often the latter period of colonialism was characterised by the re-introduction and re-enforcement of ethnicity and the 'customary' way of life by colonial authorities. Africans who had successfully become part of the colonial hierarchy were seen as being 'cheeky' and 'arrogant' and not as wholesome and reliable as the 'real', 'traditional' African. "Administrators who had begun by proclaiming their support for exploited commoners against rapacious chiefs ended by backing 'traditional' chiefly authority in the interests of social control" (1983:249). We can see a clear example of this in Transkei, where up until the mid 1950s the South African government had curbed the powers of the chiefs. Authority, which rested with the Pretoria government, was represented locally by magistrates and native commissioners (cf. Carter, Karis and Stultz, 1967). However, with the introduction of the Bantu Authorities system, local government was to be placed in the hands of the chiefs — the 'traditional' leaders of the people who for over 60 years had had virtually no official status or recognition (cf. Hammond-Tooke, 1975).

The South African government's policy of reinstating the 'traditional' role of the chiefs is, of course, not the only reason for the promotion of ethnic group formation. There is also the division of parts of South Africa into 'homelands' which is based on the official ideology that every African belongs to a particular 'ethnic group'. This ideology assumes that ethnic groupings are immutable, involuntary and homogeneous and claims that the only way to accommodate such diversity in a political framework is to assign each group to a particular geographical location. Tötemeyer (1984:45) describes the separate development policy which divides South Africa's Black population according to criteria of ethnicity, as follows —

> *It is a policy of ascribing attributes to particular groups which are expected to live and exist socially, economically and politically apart. Cultural and racial attributes are assigned to particular groups to serve as legitimation for political compartmentalisation and geographic separateness. Ethnicity has become central to the political culture dimension of authority.*

Lacey (1981:50) points out how 'homeland' divisions in themselves contribute greatly to ethnic divisiveness —

> *Ethnic divisions are deepened as competition between the bantustans over the spoils of 'independence' is stepped-up. Preferential labour agreements, 'development and investment aid', and other material incentives are basement bargains offered to bantustan authorities as rewards for their repressive roles: such tactics not only serve to deflect people's anger from the white ruling class, but in the process African solidarity in its struggle to abolish national oppression, eliminate poverty and unemployment is also being destroyed.*

Problems occur, therefore, when people do not officially 'belong' in the 'homeland' in which they find themselves. For example, in 1976, there were approximately 300 000 non-Tswana people in Bophuthatswana, the Tswana 'homeland', and in 1970, approximately 100 000 Basotho were resident in Transkei instead of in their 'homeland' — Qwa Qwa (cf. Lye and Murray, 1980:98-105). This situation results in accusations (which are often well founded) on the part of the ethnic 'foreigners' within a 'homeland', that they are discriminated against because of their ethnic identity. This state of affairs goes a long way towards explaining the increasing vehemence of ethnic animosities within these areas.

In Matatiele, ethnic awareness and identification were often expressed in terms of resentment felt by the Basotho toward the Transkeian government. Ethnicity is being used as an explanation and rationalisation for the position of powerlessness that people perceive themselves to be in. Ethnic animosity is directed primarily towards those who are seen to wield power in local affairs — for example the personnel at the magistrate's offices and agricultural offices and the nurses at the clinic. Nearly all of the civil servants at Maluti are Xhosa who usually insist upon conducting official business in Xhosa rather than Sesotho. This language problem affects mostly older Basotho villagers who claim never to have learnt Xhosa at school and never to have felt the need to learn the language. Many younger people are able to converse in Xhosa with varying degrees of fluency, but nevertheless the language barrier was felt very keenly by most Basotho and was one of the most frequently discussed 'bones of contention'. Petty forms of discrimination like this, certainly do take place on a daily basis and are the cause of a fair amount of hardship and inconvenience, but what is more, this has led to a situation where 'Xhosa-ness' is blamed for the failure of any official business that passes through Maluti (such as applications for pensions or business licenses). In addition, a government practice of sending local bureaucrats to work away from their home districts in order to cut down on nepotism, has had the effect of leading some Basotho villagers to conclude that officials are being sent far away from Matatiele **because** they are Sesotho speakers. A disgruntled pensioner who had spent many hours at Maluti trying to make herself understood in Sesotho had this to say on the subject —

> *The seniors at Maluti are Xhosas and don't want to speak Sesotho or help Sotho people. As soon as we educate our children to be clerks they send them to Umtata instead of letting them help Sotho people here in Matatiele. The only high-up Mosotho there [at Maluti] is Mr L and they are going to move him. Whenever Sotho people go there they have to look for Mr L to speak for them.*

In contrast, these language problems were never evident within St. Paul's itself. Most Xhosa residents were fluent in Sesotho; and while people did invoke ethnic stereotypes when talking about their neighbours, this was usually done with humour rather than with antagonism. For example, one day Mrs Mokoena and I were invited by friends in St. Paul's to attend a feast for a Xhosa boys' initiation ceremony which was to take place in a neighbouring village. We decided to go there on horseback but before we left we were instructed to take special care of the horses' saddles. The reason given was the 'well known' Xhosa predilection for thievery. This 'warning', related in a jocular fashion, contrasts with the far more serious accusations of unfair treatment at the hands of Xhosa clerks —

> *The clerks here at our place [Maluti] are preventing us from getting the pension. Our applications just stay at Maluti — the clerks here are Xhosas. You can never like another tribe better than your own tribe. When you go there to pay tax they tell you to speak the official language which is Xhosa. When you go there and you don't speak Xhosa they shout "thetha" which means "speak" in Xhosa and if you can't thetha you have to go away.*

Ethnicity in St. Paul's

When I first arrived in St. Paul's, it was not my intention to become involved in questions of ethnicity. However, as the months passed, it became clear that I simply could not ignore the subject. So many responses to questions about local government and Transkeian 'independence' were phrased in terms of ethnicity, that it became obvious that not to investigate the issue further would be to leave a serious gap in the picture of people's perceptions of the Transkeian state. Conversely, as Cohen (1974a), emphasises, ethnicity itself has to be studied in the light of its connections with economics and politics. For whilst ethnicity may at first sight appear to be formally unrelated to politics, closer examination always reveals a highly politicised situation. In this instance, the resort to accusations of ethnic prejudice must be seen in the context of an ethnically constituted 'homeland', where those who wield power are associated with a particular ethnic identity.

So, when I completed my village census towards the end of my stay, I decided to collect information about ethnic self-identification. It is necessary, at this point, to stress the words 'ethnic self-identification' and to emphasise that my aim was not to impute a neat set of cultural labels. In addition, it must be noted that informants were talking to me — an outsider and anthropologist — and were often keen to stress ethnic differences for my benefit and probably far more than was usual amongst friends and neighbours.

My first impressions of St. Paul's were that it was fairly ethnically homogeneous. Then I noticed that some people spoke Xhosa and that the Xhosa-speaking women wore distinctive head-dresses, and in addition, there was sometimes a notable difference in the way Xhosas decorated the exterior of their houses. Naturally, at such functions as the celebrations for the Xhosa boys' initiation rites, Xhosa identity was publicly demonstrated and stressed. During the months of December and January, the longest school holiday, many young people were away at initiation lodges. Their return was a time not only for celebrations, but also of much discussion in the village about the subject of initiation. Villagers were very keen to explain the 'true facts' to me, their visitor, in case I did not understand what was happening, and during these talks individual's ethnic identities were usually established. Thus people would explain to me similarities between Basotho and Hlubi by pointing out that Hlubi boys attended Sotho initiation rites and similarly they would make hazy reference to the differences between Sotho and Xhosa rites, stressing what they considered to be the shortcomings in each other's practices. It is significant to note that the first-ever Xhosa initiation to be held in St. Paul's took place soon after my arrival in the village and I was not the only curious onlooker at this event. Up until that time, the very small number of Xhosa families in the village had not warranted a local initiation school, and Xhosa youths had been sent to other villages in the district for this purpose.

So by the time of my census, I already had a fair idea of people's ethnic identity and usually phrased my questions in terms of asking for confirmation of this identity. Women who were, or had been, married to someone of a different ethnic background were usually quick to point out that their children had a different ethnic identity to themselves, i.e. that of their husbands. The information presented in the table below was collected from each household in St. Paul's and refers to the identity claimed by adult members of the household. Usually the **de facto** head of the household was interviewed. This information is not exhaustive; it does not, for example, include visitors to households or employees temporarily residing with employers; nor does it include all marriages within households. For example, the Mokoenas (comprising a Mosotho husband and Hlubi wife) employed a Xhosa servant who shared their home; and one of their neighbours had their Xhosa son and Sotho daughter-in-law staying with them until they could find a place of their own. However, the table does give a broad indication of the proportions of stated ethnic identity.

STATED ETHNIC IDENTITIES OF VILLAGE HOUSEHOLDS

Sotho	116
Xhosa	.15
Hlubi	. 9
'Mixed marriages'*	.22
Total	162

* The 'mixed marriages' comprised: 12 unions between Basotho and Hlubi; 5 between Basotho and Xhosa; and 5 between individuals of other ethnic identities (e.g. Bhaca and Zulu).

The core of St. Paul's villagers — 124 households — came to the village in 1969-71, as a result of the 'betterment' scheme described in Chapter One. The majority of these people were Basotho, but there were also a number of Hlubi families. Most of the new-comers who joined the village **after** this resettlement are Xhosas who moved to St. Paul's at different times from other parts of the district in search of land. This would explain why slightly more of the 'mixed marriages' in the village have taken place between Sotho and Hlubi people, who in the main have grown up together, and in most instances were resettled from the same place in Ramohlakoana.

According to the Transkei's 1980 census, Ramohlakoana location is populated by 1 111 Xhosa people and 3 289 people who belong to "other groups". However, the census figures show that the district of Matatiele as a whole has a clear majority of Xhosas — 68 359 as opposed to 31 115 members of "other groups". Nevertheless, a number of Basotho villagers claim that Matatiele district is predominantly Sotho and therefore should not be part of Transkei. Spiegel (1982), in fact, queries these census figures and suggests that the margin of Xhosa majority is exaggerated and that there are more Basotho in the area than the Transkeian government wishes to acknowledge. Save for carrying out one's own census, it is impossible to achieve greater clarity on this point, but it does seem safe to say that the Basotho do form a significant presence in the district but do not constitute a majority.

Sotho Historical Claims to the District

A more popular justification than the numerical claim to the district was the historical explanation quoted by a number of Basotho villagers. According to this line of thought, Matatiele district should not be subject to the iniquities of 'Xhosa government' because the area had been settled by Basotho in the 1860s and Xhosas were relative new-comers. Weber (1978 edition) pointed out that a group's self-consciousness is often based on a belief in common descent which may be real or imagined, as well as on common cultural traits. Therefore, the expression of ethnic identity is only meaningful when different groups come into contact with one another and a situation arises where it becomes relevant to accentuate cultural differences between 'us' and 'them'. The creation of ethnicity is thus a "political artifact" (Weber, 1978:393) which may be used to mobilise action; and customs and cultural traits are easily subject to manipulation when either 'affinity' or 'disaffinity' between two groups is to be stressed. Parsons (1975:56) also stresses the importance of belief in common origins for people's perceptions of their ethnic identity. He defines an ethnic group as one where — "members . . . have, both with respect to their own sentiments and those of non-members, a distinctive identity which is rooted in some kind of a distinctive sense of its history". Most importantly then, we must realise that ethnic boundaries are not fixed and immutable, but that the emergence of ethnic identity is a dynamic response to specific situations. The oral histories which were quoted to me by many villagers (both old and young) illustrate the way that people are able to invoke a sense of their historical claim, as **Basotho**, to Matatiele.

Many a villager would tell me that Matatiele is a "Sotho place" because "our forefather Lepheana trekked here with Adam Kok," and it was often explained to me how Queen Victoria had had 'mercy' and given the Basotho some land — hence the place-name 'Queen's Mercy' (see map 3). Often oral histories were detailed and consistent with one another and were produced as 'proof' whenever I questioned the claim that Matatiele is a 'Sotho place'. As one informant put it —

The Basotho are not living happily under the Xhosas, because the Basotho were given this place to be the chiefs over it. It was given to them by Adam Kok, Lepheana said the place belonged to Bahlokoana [name of the chiefly clan]. We are unhappy because the Xhosas have made their town at Maluti and are unhappy with the way they treat us.

The pertinent historical points about Adam Kok's **trek** to Nomansland in the company of Lepheana, are described in Chapter One above. Below I give three local accounts of that history, which all, despite slight differences, dwell upon the fact that the Basotho have an historical claim to the land in and around current-day Ramohlakoana location.

1.   When the Basotho first came here, they came with Adam Kok, that was in the 1860s. Lepheana, the father of Ramohlakoana, joined with Kok in Basutoland. Adam Kok gave Lepheana land from the Umzimvubu to the Drakensburg. Lepheana settled on Malubelube hill just below it overlooking Matatiele and his sons were also given land. Sibi also came with Kok and was given separate land by him.

2.   This area belongs to the Basotho historically and logically. The Basotho people came here with the Griquas in the last century and they were the first. At that time this place was called Nomansland and it was empty. Why should the Basotho go and live in Lesotho or Qwa Qwa when Matatiele is our home?

3.   This place used to be called Nomansland until Adam Kok and his Griquas came here. Adam Kok, Adam; invited our forefather Lepheana to accompany him and he gave him land to be chief over it. All of this land along the Kinira River up to the mountains was given to the Bahlakoana and this was a Sotho place. But now Matanzima said that it's one nation. It would be nice if we could have our separate Sotho government at Ramohlakoana.

It is interesting to note that contemporary villagers made no mention, in their accounts, of the rivalry and conflict that took place (especially in the 1870s) between Lepheana's following and that of Nehemiah Moshesh, (see Chapter One above). Bardsley (1982) points out that the significant political tensions in Nomansland were not to be found between the Mfengu — of whom there were a significant number (cf. Ross, 1974:137) — and the Basotho, but rather between the two Sotho factions —

The dominant theme is, rather, the strain between the 'Moshesh' faction on the one hand, represented by Nehemiah and later Makoae and his son Sekake, and the 'Mapheana' faction represented by patriarch Lepheana and sons Ramohlakoana, Mosi, Marthinus and Sibi. There were reasons for this hostility in old Lesotho disputes (Bardsley, 1982:57).

As pointed out above, some people mentioned that Queen's Mercy was a 'gift' from Queen Victoria to loyal **Basotho**, but the fact that this was land granted to the rival Moshesh faction was never raised. This convenient omission underlines the necessity for viewing ethnicity in its political context; historical details of Sotho rivalry have no place in accounts which aim to stress the Basotho historical claim to the area. By contrast, Xhosa villagers referred to the fact of their numerical superiority in Transkei as justification for being in Matatiele (in this case in St. Paul's). They shrugged off the idea of a Basotho historical claim and suggested that Sotho people should move if they were not happy in Transkei. According to one Xhosa resident in St. Paul's —

> *Matanzima has said that he doesn't want tribalism, they can speak their own languages but these Sothos must know that they are under a Xhosa government. It's a lie that Xhosas oppress Sothos. Some people like to complain. They are just jealous of the Xhosa government — they were told that if they didn't like to be under XG [Xhosa government] they could take their things and go — if they want to go to Lesotho they can go.*

Many of these sentiments were expressed in formal terms in the period just prior to 'independence', in 1976, when Basotho politicians lobbied for the secession of the Maluti region (comprising Matatiele and Mount Fletcher) and Herschel to Qwa Qwa. Southall (1983:141) reports that the secessionists also suggested joining Lesotho or remaining as part of South Africa. The Chief Minister of Qwa Qwa, Kenneth Mopeli took the occasion of Transkei's 'independence' as an opportunity to demand more land from the South African government for his small impoverished 'national state' and to wax rhetorical about the fate of Basotho living in Transkei. He pointed to the inconsistency in South African government policy that "condemned" Basotho to live in a 'homeland' governed not by their own ethnic group, and as Transkeian 'independence' grew near, "[T]he Qwaqwa cabinet . . . called on South Sotho nationals to regard Transkei Independence Day as a day of mourning for more than 40 000 of their people who would become 'enslaved' in Transkei on land that **historically** belonged to the South Sotho" (my emphasis, Streek and Wicksteed, 1981:51).

These events, coupled with the detention in 1976 of three local Basotho politicians who voiced opposition to inclusion in 'independent' Transkei, and the arrests of others accused of being 'involved in politics', have contributed to two current attitudes amongst local villagers. Firstly, as I have already mentioned elsewhere, people harbour a dread of becoming involved in any kind of formal politics outside the legitimacy of TNIP meetings. This fear often manifests itself as a reluctance to complain or voice grievances to officials at any level of the government hierarchy. Local TNIP officials are at pains to stress to villagers that the best channel for their complaints is their local TNIP branch. This has led people to assume that protest and complaint, no matter how mild, is being 'political', and the arrests of 1976 (although none were from St. Paul's itself) are still relatively fresh in people's memories. This, of course, does not prevent people from complaining vociferously about the government amongst themselves. Sometimes issues like the appalling state of the village roads or the fact that some villagers still did not have their pensions or a new levy that was being demanded to pay for school construction, would be discussed at the village **pitso**. Those present would say that the government was killing them with all the taxes they required, that people had no money and that they would gladly fix their own roads if the government would pay them for their labour. These complaints rarely got any further than this. The headman, old, tired and scared, tried not to get involved and individuals were also nervous about complaining for fear that they would make their circumstances worse. Often I was asked to intervene on people's behalf and help them face the hostile bureaucracy at Maluti.

Secondly, the antagonism that local Basotho feel towards the Transkeian government is couched largely in ethnic terms, the blame for problems being laid at the door of "Matanzima's bloody Xhosas". The reason, it is argued, that the roads in Matatiele are in disrepair, is because Matatiele is a Sotho place, and the reason that old people cannot get their pensions is because the **Xhosa** clerks do not send away the application forms filled in by Basotho.

The political activity that led up to the arrests in 1976 was confined to a few educated people, members of what I have called the elite group, or 'seniors' to use the local term. However, although most ordinary villagers were not involved in any political protest at the time, and by their own accounts were not (and still are not) fully aware of the issue in question, they still talk of the affair and maintain a lively awareness of the Basotho historical claim to Matatiele. These factors also contribute to the sentiment expressed by many that Matatiele district should have remained part of South Africa at the time of Transkei's 'independence', South African rule being perceived as far preferable to a Xhosa government.

Are Basotho Allegations of Discrimination Justified?

The stories of ethnic discrimination that were related to me by Basotho villagers were usually tales of bureaucratic inefficiency and callousness experienced by people at Maluti. The ethnic element is one way of rationalising and explaining the situation and ethnic explanations can be changed and manipulated to suit the occasion. Thus, Mrs Matsosa, a Hlubi, blames government inefficiency on the behaviour of Basotho themselves, saying that because of their timidity and stupidity they never speak up and let their case be known to the authorities. "The Hlubis and Xhosas" she claims, "are the leaders because those Basotho are scared to talk out and so they lose their power. They like to talk a lot, but when they **should** talk, they fail!" Her Xhosa friend also had very fixed ideas about her Basotho neighbours —

Basotho are all the same — they complain all the time. Even when they are welcomed nicely they just complain until they quarrel amongst themselves. It would be a good idea for Basotho to have their own place — they could make their problems by themselves then. Some Basotho are nice, but they need a long time for things to be explained to them.

However, she protested in the same way as almost everyone else did about the shoddy treatment received at the administrative centre — "here at Maluti these high rank people are very selfish — when you go to pay tax, you wait there till the bus has left you while these people discuss their personal matters". A slightly different interpretation was given to the question by a Hlubi businessman who was of the opinion that Basotho are discriminated against by the government. He believes that Matatiele district is neglected as far as development is concerned, which makes life more difficult for him as a businessman. "Yes, it's true that I'm a Hlubi," he said, "but I'm living amongst Basotho, so in their [the government's] eyes I'm just the same as them!" These sorts of data illustrate quite clearly that the main lines of deep antagonism are really drawn between ordinary villagers and the Transkeian government personified by its local representatives. The main reason for this being, that while there is a range of economic differentiation within St. Paul's, individuals do not gain any great material benefits by virtue of their ethnic affiliation. So, at present Xhosa and Basotho villagers alike find themselves equally constrained by government corruption and inefficiency.

Cohen is most insistent in his view that examining culture or customs alone sheds no light on the contemporary situation in which they are being practised. The important issue is **why** certain customs have survived, disappeared or been revived and how their functions have changed. Says Cohen (1974b:4), "[W]ithin the contemporary situation ethnicity is essentially a political phenomenon, as traditional customs are only used as idioms and as mechanisms for political alignments". The crux of his theorising lies in the relation between what he calls 'symbolic action', that is the practice of cultural traits, and power relationships (in other words, politics). His emphasis is squarely on the way that people exploit their ethnic identity to further their own ends. If it is in people's interest to rally themselves around the common banner of their ethnic identity, then other 'war cries' — like the solidarity of the working class — will be ignored. Cohen adds that (1974b:17) "[C]lasses are the figments of the imagination of sociologists" and that society is really made up of a **series** of interest groups who choose from a variety of ways of organising themselves. By the same token we may add that neatly bounded ethnic groups are also figments of the imagination. This is certainly the situation in St. Paul's where people choose to emphasise or ignore ethnic identity according to the particular context.

In considering these issues it might be useful to borrow a concept from the field of medical anthropology — that of a hierarchy of resort (cf. Janzen, 1978) whereby patients 'resort' to different kinds of therapy, choosing the one that they believe will be the most effective and abandoning those which do not work. Accepting that ethnic group formation is dynamic and purposive in nature and that a fascinating area of interest is the resurgence or revival of old cultural forms, around which people identify themselves (Cohen's symbolic action), then we must ask at what **level of resort** does this kind of behaviour occur? In order to answer this question we must examine the particular context of group formation, bearing in mind Cohen's point that people rally around their ethnic identity because it is to their own advantage, or that they are rallied together to serve the purposes of some behind-the-scenes manipulators. In other words we should constantly remind ourselves that people rarely practise exotic customs for the benefit of ethnographers or because they are conservative or nostalgic, but rather for specific purposes. Burgess (1978:267) comments that ethnicity can be seen as ". . . a rational group response to social pressures and a basis for group action, especially where none other exists".

Manona's (1980) examination of ethnic tensions in Burnshill and Nyaniso in Ciskei is illustrative of these points. Manona traces ethnic animosity between Xhosa and Mfengu back to the nineteenth century, particularly to the fact that the Mfengu aided the British colonists during the frontier wars which ended in 1879. As a result of their 'loyalty' to the colony, Mfengu were rewarded with land at the expense of the Xhosa. In the two settlements where Manona did research he found that the long-standing **land-owning** residents were usually Mfengu, whereas the newcomers who had no land were, in the main, Xhosa. Tension and conflict arose between the two groups and was expressed in terms of ethnic differences, senti-ments which Manona argues had not been given expression since the 1920s. He attributes this resurgence to "competition for scarce resources especially land" and the fact that this competition is fought in terms of ethnicity to —

> . . . the system of Bantu Authorities which on the one hand encouraged the ideology of ethnicity and on the other hand opened new avenues for a struggle for power. In fact, the policy of separate development, based as it is on the recognition of exclusive ethnic units, has contributed a great deal to these ethnic conflicts (1980:119).

Similarly, James (1985) describes the ethnic tensions that emerged when a community in Lebowa staged a protest against a government agricultural scheme. The community comprised both Pedi and Ndebele speakers but it was the Pedi speakers who were most vociferous in their complaints against the agricultural co-operative. However, once again there was a situation where the core group of long-standing residents who had access to land were Ndebele speakers and in addition, the chief under whose jurisdiction the community fell was Ndebele. By virtue of their longer period of residence in the area the Ndebele had consolidated themselves through links of marriage and in one sample of landholding Ndebele, 57% were related by kinship ties to the chief (1985:28). So when plotholders (comprising both Pedi and Ndebele, but with a majority of the latter) staged their protest, the chief was able to exert his authority and defuse the situation. However the "deferential and obedient attitude to their chief" angered the Pedi and added to their resentment of a chief who they claimed favoured Ndebele in the allocation of land (1985:25-26). James concludes by saying that —

> *In the light of the development in other Bantustan situations, in which competition over scarce resources has led to increased ethnic conflict, it may be that similar divisions will plague future attempts by . . . farmers to express their indignation at outside interference with their use of the land (1985:31).*

At the moment there are no such clear-cut divisions in St. Paul's because there are very few material resources within the village for which individuals could compete. However, I would suggest that a parallel situation could arise quite easily were it to appear, for example, that newly arrived Xhosa residents were given preference on the waiting list for residential plots or for fields. Strong sentiments in this regard are already being voiced by a number of Basotho, for example Mrs Selekhiso said the following —

> *There is less land here in Matatiele because lots of people — Xhosas — came here in a big number during the time of Moliko [the previous chief]. Moliko has made big trouble for us by letting these Xhosas squash us — they are also thieves — they steal cattle and sheep . . . These people come here and get sites here in our place and now their sons will be getting the new sites. Most of these Xhosas are on the waiting lists for the new sites and when the new sites are opened up . . . they will get them. These Xhosas may give the appearance of being Basotho — because they speak Sesotho and take on the Sotho customs. They are very clever, these Xhosas because they try by all means to make friends with us and practise Sotho customs so that we won't make them leave.*

In fact this fluidity of ethnic identity is clearly demonstrated by Hlubi villagers who choose to identify themselves either as being closer to the 'Sotho culture' or the 'Xhosa culture' as occasion demands. Mrs Mokoena was, herself, a very good example of this. She is a Hlubi who has married into a Sotho family and, having grown up in the environment of Ramohlakoana location and then spent many years working as a domestic servant in Johannesburg, she speaks fluent Sesotho as well as Hlubi and Xhosa. When in the company of her Basotho neighbours (and especially in the context of discussing ethnicity as my interpreter) Mrs Mokoena would stress the common features of Hlubi and Sotho culture. She, and others in mixed Hlubi/Basotho company, would talk about the similarity of their customs and would invoke unflattering ethnic stereotypes about Xhosas, how untrustworthy and dishonest they are especially in comparison with themselves. Conversely, when Hlubis and Xhosas were present, Hlubis were able to point out the closeness of the their two languages and talk about the simple mindedness of their Basotho neighbours.

Interestingly, although Xhosas and Hlubis are very much in the minority, they usually hold leading posts in village clubs and organisations. Of the headman's committee, the school committee, the **zenzele** (women's self-help group) committee, the TNIP committee and the mealie-meal aid committee, all were dominated by Xhosas and Hlubis with the exception of the headman's committee. This was also the case in two out of the three funeral associations in St. Paul's. Sometimes this may be by virtue of the fact that certain officials are appointed by the 'Xhosa government', for example, the village ranger who is responsible for the condition of local fences and boundary gates, amongst other things. In other instances local groups, such as funeral associations and school committees, find it to their advantage to elect Xhosa-speaking chairpersons. In this way the group is assured of a leading representative, who, if needs be will be able to communicate pin the official language at Maluti. Be that as it may, individuals insist in private on resorting to well-used stereotypes: Basotho maintain that Xhosas achieve important positions through their lies, cheating and cunning, while Xhosas claim that Basotho never get anywhere because they are stupid, lazy and talk too much. However, despite these insults, it must be stressed that within the village people of all ethnic backgrounds live quite amicably together and during the period of my stay, no disputes were publicly contested along ethnic lines. The facts that Basotho, Xhosa and Hlubi voluntarily belong to the same clubs, have friendships with one another and intermarry, show that animosity between them does not run as deep as many individuals maintain. However, people in the village, with the exception of a very few, were united in the resentment that they felt towards the government, and for Basotho villagers the added dimension of ethnicity contributed extra fire to their indignation. It is not difficult to see how this comes about: take for example the following case which deals with the local dipping tank.

Taking one's cattle to be dipped is an important chore for stockowners. Government regulations require cattle to be taken to government dipping tanks once a fortnight in summer and once a month in winter. The penalty for non-compliance is a fine and the possibility of having cattle impounded. St. Paul's villagers have to take their cattle to a dipping tank situated about an hour's walk from the village, which makes the whole procedure a tiring and time- consuming duty. Cattle-owners in the village were thus keen to get permission to rebuild an old dipping tank situated just across the road from St. Paul's which had originally been built and used by the church people from the mission station. The first applications for a new dipping tank near the village were made soon after 'independence' by a villager who was able to speak Xhosa, the headman at the time being a Sesotho speaker only. Permission to rebuild the old mission dipping tank was eventually received in 1982, but the cost of the operation was to be borne by the villagers themselves. Accordingly, R1 was collected from each cattle-owner and the village men completed the work themselves. Stock inspectors from the local agricultural offices were said to have come and approved the job, but at the time of my stay the dipping tank was still not being used by the stock inspectors, and people were still obliged to walk kilometres to have their cattle dipped. The enclosure around the tank itself was rapidly falling into disrepair and weeds were beginning to force their way through cracks in the cement. The blame for this state of affairs is not merely attributed to local bureaucratic inefficiency, but is seen by men involved with the building project as a deliberate Xhosa plot. Said one man,

> *The stock inspectors are from Maluti and are all Xhosas. They ill-treat us here, they don't bring jobs to the village, like fixing roads and filling in dongas. Near Umtata where they are all Xhosas, people are always earning money doing those jobs. We are still waiting for them to open our dipping tank, in the meantime people have to walk many miles. . . The Xhosas want the Basotho to be under them because they are in the government. The Basotho here in Matat. should have their own government.*

The reason that the dipping tank has not been opened may well be because the stock inspectors and their superiors have some grudge against Basotho villagers, but given an environment where bureaucratic inefficiency is rife, this hardly seems likely. A more likely explanation may be found in the very common human trait of needing an individual or group on whom to place the blame for one's misfortunes. This tendency is very well illustrated by the attitudes and opinions that people have about the Tribal Authority. Disillusionment with the degree of corruption and injustice at the Tribal Authority runs high and is a constant cause for complaint. As I mentioned in Chapter One, the Tribal Authority is able to wield a certain amount of control over people's lives. For example, applications to improve roads, build schools, acquire plots, are ultimately approved or disapproved either at the offices at Maluti or in Umtata. Yet, before those applications can be taken to Maluti they have to pass through the hands of the headman and the Tribal Authority and be approved by them. People's complaints and applications often get 'stuck' at this preliminary stage unless appropriate bribes are paid. Often at this local level personal animosities and grievances are paid back, even making bribing impossible. Here individual personalities manipulate the system to their own advantage, motivated by the attainment of more power within the local government structure which ultimately leads to greater wealth.

Descriptions of the machinations and shortcomings of the Tribal Authority cannot be couched in ethnic terms as the body is made up of predominantly Basotho members. However, it is not uncommon to hear people attribute corruption at the Tribal Authority to mental instability within the chiefly clan. This claim is supported to some extent by the fact that there have been a number of cases of mental illness in the chief's immediate family. Be that as it may, these allegations do lead one to suspect that accusations of ethnic prejudice and discrimination may often be exaggerated.

I do not want to give the impression, however, that Basotho in St. Paul's are suffering from some kind of persecution complex and that they have created in the Xhosa government some kind of scapegoat for their grievances (although this viewpoint is not entirely without justification). There were many occasions when I witnessed for myself discrimination directed at Basotho. Local officialdom, in fact, seems bent on deliberately ignoring the existence of Basotho in the area. At official meetings I attended this was made graphically obvious in the way that Xhosa chiefs from locations at the other side of the district were invited to attend, while local Basotho dignitaries were conspicuous by their absence. At the official opening of the already three year old Maluti Health Centre, at which the Minister of Health presided, the crowd was addressed as — "loyal Xhosas and Hlubis". This was despite the obvious fact that those present were predominantly Basotho (as already mentioned, even the 1980 census shows that both Ramohlakoana, where the gathering was being held, and neighbouring Khoapa location have significant Basotho majorities). Most speeches were made in English and translated into Xhosa and so were not understood by many of the older people present.

At the same time as these sorts of gestures seem designed to show the locals that they are indeed under a **Xhosa** government, there seem to have been recent official efforts to de-emphasise ethnic differences and to assert first and foremost Transkeian identity. This is the message conveyed by the local government delegates (or 'delicates' as they have come to be known as a result of a mispronunciation) at regional and village TNIP meetings. At a district TNIP gathering at which everything from bribery and government inefficiency to cattle theft and diet at boarding-schools was mulled over (this of course being the legitimate place for making these observations) one of the 'delicates' made the following statement. He was answering the question asked at most TNIP meetings which is — "what is TNIP and of what use is it?"

> *You are asking many questions about — what is TNIP? — now the answer is this: Most of the people do not know what* **Imbumba** *[the party rallying cry, literally translated as 'unity'] is.* **Imbumba** *changes the 13 tribes of Transkei into one nation. All of you have equal rights just as you have the light of TNIP . . . There should be no more tribalism. Everyone should look in their Book of Life and they will see that there is no one called a Sotho or a Hlubi etc. like in the old days, it just says Transkeian.*

These kinds of statements presumably come as a response to inter-ethnic problems that erupted in Transkei during 1983 and 1984, particularly in the Lusikisiki and Tabankulu areas in the south.

It is also interesting to note that in February, 1984, a new post was created at Maluti — that of an officer for Information and Foreign Affairs. His job, he told me, was one of liaison between the government and the people, and he aimed to ease local tensions and misunderstandings. After expounding the Transkeian government's views on nationalism, he confided that he believed that the region's and country's (Transkei) problems centre around ethnicity and he expressed despondency about ever resolving these issues. He himself seemed torn between the government line of nationalism and non-tribalism, and his personal convictions about the integrity of maintaining one's own customs in the face of the destructive elements of a 'Western lifestyle'. This was a dilemma voiced by many and will be a theme which I shall be taking up in Chapter Five.

Conclusion

The data that I collected, illustrated most forcefully the very fluid and malleable nature of ethnicity itself. As Weber himself conceded, the term 'ethnic group' has no precise referent; it is ambiguous for the very reason that the groups themselves are not concrete or fixed, but are constantly subject to flux. Not only may cultural traits and customs change over time, but also the emphases placed on their importance vary with context and situation. So ". . . the concept of the 'ethnic' group . . . dissolves if we define our terms exactly . . ." (Weber, 1978:395). This is borne out by the situation in St. Paul's where it is not possible to draw sharp lines of ethnic boundary, for people may choose to accentuate their ethnic identities on some occasions but not on others. If groups **can** be identified, then there are two broad categories. One group comprises local government officials (and this would include members of the Tribal Authority) and those people who have benefited from the 'independence' of Transkei. For example, the teachers and entrepreneurs, who along with the bureaucrats are identified by Charton (1976) and Southall (1977; 1983) as being Transkei's modern elites (cf. Chapter Two above). In the other category we find practically all of the villagers whose major day-to-day concerns are those of subsistence and survival. It is quite clear that as a result of the South African government's policy of dividing people and allocating them to various 'homelands', using criteria of ethnicity, the people themselves tend to think of the 'homeland' governments in ethnic terms. Being a Mosotho under a proclaimed Xhosa government already heightens awareness amongst people of ethnic differences. Add to this situation the kinds of discrimination described above, particularly those connected with language problems (language probably being the most significant indicator of ethnicity in the area) and the context of general village poverty, and we have an environment in which the resort to accusations of ethnic discrimination is logical. Ethnicity in this instance provides people with explanations for their position in the social order and can be emphasised or ignored as the situation demands. As Isaacs (1975:30) comments — "It [ethnicity] is the refuge to which . . . great masses are retreating and withdrawing in the face of the breakdown or inadequacy of all the larger coherences or systems of power and social organization".

CHAPTER 5

THE SIGNIFICANCE OF CUSTOM

The practice of customs is a subject which has traditionally received attention from anthropologists; and opportunity for such study is not lacking in St. Paul's where initiation rites, feasts for the ancestors, marriage celebrations (to name a few instances) take place quite regularly. However, we need to question the degree to which these practices constitute a direct continuity with the past and to examine their persistence — and in some cases their revival — in the particular political context of a Transkeian village. Once more it will become evident that the practice of certain customs often has a political dimension, and that individuals may manipulate the prevailing cultural idiom to suit their own purposes. Similarly, the revival or maintenance of customary practice has to be seen against a background where ordinary villagers find their participation in formal politics to be frustrating and unsatisfying and where the government, or its local agents, are often perceived to be working against people's interests. In this contemporary situation, the past and the customs associated with it, are often imbued with a certain romance and are viewed with nostalgia.

Here I am trying once more to look at the **individual's** motives for, and responses to, certain customary practices, and to ask why some people should be so enthusiastic as to spend time, money and energy on the maintenance of customs like initiation, especially in the context of a community which aspires to the 'Western lifestyle' which is so vigorously promoted in nearby Matatiele town.

If the theme of Chapter Four was predominantly that of how Basotho villagers perceive themselves to be in a disadvantaged position as a result of their ethnic identity, then a theme which emerges strongly here, is the position of marginality that almost all ordinary villagers find themselves in. Their marginality is that of people who find that their poverty excludes them from access to a range of goods and activities to which they aspire. I have already discussed, in Chapter One, how the proximity of St. Paul's to Matatiele town places it in a 'betwixt and between' situation with villagers constantly being bombarded with advertising propaganda. But financial pressures make it more and more difficult for the majority to attain the luxuries and trappings associated with the lifestyle of the Whites.

Initiation — a Quaint and Colourful Custom?

Mayer (1971) discusses the persistence of 'traditional' manhood initiation in the urban environment of Port Elizabeth. He notes that while the initiation ceremony has retained much of its outward formal structure, attitudes towards it have undergone significant change. These attitudinal differences, he suggests, are indicative of social change and are not only applicable to the practice of initiation.

> *It could be said of many other 'traditional' institutions, as of Xhosa initiation, that people continue to do the thing as before but it no longer means the same as before. Such a proposition raises theoretical questions about functions, 'meanings', values and norms or the relations between attitudes and actions (Mayer, 1971:9).*

It is imperative to view the persistence of custom in the context of contemporary political and social conditions if such practices are not to be designated as irrational adherence to a set of archaic traditions. Murray (1977; 1980a; 1981) argues this point most forcefully with particular reference to the continued practice of bride-wealth payments on the South African rural periphery despite the breakdown of family life. He points out that although high bridewealth payments exist in Lesotho today as they did a century ago, the current practice is by no means the same. The payment of high bridewealth in the mid-nineteenth century helped to consolidate and centralise the power of the chiefs, members of the aristocratic Koena clan. Their access to large numbers of cattle enabled them to practise polygyny and hence to expand in numbers very rapidly as well as to sponsor a client-following by lending out cattle for the puposes of bridewealth payments (Murray, 1977:81). In contemporary Lesotho, however, bridewealth has to be understood in relation to the migrant labour system. Marriages are almost all monogamous and bridewealth transactions legitimise children ensuring future access to cash remittances when adult children in turn become migrants, as well as future income in the form of bridewealth itself. Bridewealth payments have thus become investments in the next generation, ". . . mechanism[s] by which migrants invest in the long-term security of the rural social system, and by which rural kin constitute claims over absent earners" (Murray, 1981:148).

In contrast to Murray's work, Hammond-Tooke (1981) sets out to document and "interpret" the world-view of the Kgaga — Sesotho-speakers who live in the Lowveld. He specifically excludes any mention of the broader social and political context saying that "[A] detailed discussion of the present-day political system will not be attempted here as it is only marginally relevant to the theme of this study" (1981:26). The result must surely be that we are only presented with **part** of these people's "world-view", for, as Hammond-Tooke explains, initiation serves to incorporate young people into the "politico-jural domain" (p.36), "maintain the integrity of their social structure" (p. 35) and teach "the values of good citizenship"

(p. 82). He also mentions that many Kgaga practise Christianity (p. vii), that the area has been subjected to a government rehabilitation scheme (p. 4) and he presents photographs of Kgaga wearing factory-made clothing. Clearly, Kgaga experience extends beyond the confines of the Kgaga chiefdom and a full understanding of, for example, Kgaga initiation rites can only be achieved by examining the much broader political, economic and social situation.

So too, the continued practice of male initiation rites and the revival of female initiation in St. Paul's must be examined in the context of 'independent' Transkei.

Initiation of boys has, according to informants, gained in popularity in the area in recent times — "before only a few people were getting initiated, now most of the young boys know they will be going to initiation". During the long December (1983) school holidays three lots of boys were initiated in St. Paul's alone, and in and around the village the number of boys smeared with red oxide and wearing red blankets, indicative of their newly initiated status, was striking.

There was no suggestion that male initiation had ever died out in the area and was now being revived, but by most accounts the practice is now being received with more enthusiasm than it was some years ago. It is interesting to note that Ashton, who did field research in the mid 1930s, had this to say on the subject of initiation —

> A hundred years ago, initiation was probably the most important ceremonial institution of the Basuto, but to-day it is rapidly breaking down . . . Elsewhere in Basutoland it is almost dead and it is only in the foothills that it is still occasionally held. Its decay is due mainly to missionary influence and to the inevitable change in Basuto ideas as a result of European contact (1952:55).

He also speaks of the 'traditional inducements' necessary to force reluctant schoolboys to go to the initiation lodge —

> The need for bolstering the traditional "inducements", especially nowadays, when the opposition of schools, Christianity and the principal chiefs has strengthened boys' fear and reluctance to face initiation, is clearly shown by the case of my young helper . . . he was wildly excited by the . . . lure of the lodge and the excitement of its ceremonies, and he longed for the day when he would be old enough to go. But four or five years later, when his turn came, he was enjoying school and was so much afraid of being expelled if he went to the initiation lodge that he ran away from home and had to be forcibly brought back and pushed into the lodge (1952:47).

In St. Paul's I found a situation where parents did not complain that their sons did not want to go to the initiation lodges, but rather that young boys — from the age of about 12 years — were running away, without warning, to join initiation schools. Most parents (especially fathers) expressed approval of male initiation, but were mildly annoyed if their sons ran away without telling them because of the unexpected expense involved. The cost to the boy's family could be as much as R250, comprising such items as a sheep, mealie meal, **jwala** (home-brewed beer), new blankets, knobkerrie, fee for the **mosue** (teacher), etc.

Another indication that initiation now enjoys greater popularity and significance in the area is the fact that a few older male teachers (in their forties and fifties) were recently forcibly abducted and taken to be initiated. For it was not fitting that uninitiated men should teach initiated children at school.

A large percentage of boys in St. Paul's have attended initiation schools. Of the **131** males aged between 15 and 25 years, **89** (68%) of them had already been initiated, with eight more planning to go in the near future. However, the parents of 12 of the boys in this age group were vehemently opposed to their sons being initiated, the main reason being strong religious belief. Nevertheless, many parents of young children expressed the desire to send their sons to be initiated when they came of age, although many qualified these statements by saying that they wanted their boys to become educated first. As one mother put it —

> *People should send their children to initiation, but school is number one. They should go to initiation when they are old enough and reasoning, like when they are 18 years old. Education is necessary for getting work, but initiation is the custom — others have become sick or mentally disturbed but after initiation they become okay.*

It must be recognised that as a woman **and** as an outsider, I experienced difficulties in collecting data on male initiations. However, asking questions about the reasons for, and importance of, initiation was less problematic than talking about or attending specific initiation ceremonies. Nevertheless, young men themselves were usually reluctant to talk to me about initiation and conversations on the subject would be punctuated with embarrassed laughter. Many said that they intended going for initiation because their friends had been and — "a man cannot stay happily with his friends if they are all initiated and he is not". Even the boys who said that they did not want to go to the initiation lodge, but were more interested in furthering their formal education said that they would like to go to the doctor in town to be circumcised — for "health reasons". However, most boys were of the opinion that unless one goes to an initiation lodge in the mountains, one is not a "real man". Older men were even more reticent on the subject, but would say that initiation was a boy's "real" education making him tough and strong. Initiation schools were often referred to as "bush universities" or "high schools", and were spoken of almost as finishing schools where young men received education which was complementary to the skills of literacy learnt in the formal education system, but which did not fully equip them for the rigours of a working life away from home. In fact in the context of rising unemployment and increasing inefficiency in Transkeian schools (see Chapter Two above), there is a growing realisation that formal education alone is not the guarantee of employment that people used to perceive it to be. As I have mentioned before, there is a tendency amongst people to associate growing unemployment and lack of mining contracts at the TEBA offices with Transkeian 'independence'. This association is further rationalised and justified by the claim that even when children do succeed in their school examinations, they are further disadvantaged by the fact that they have **Transkeian** school certificates.

> *Our children must pull very hard because on their certificates is written* **Imbumba ya Manyama** *['Unity is Strength' — the official Transkeian motto]. The ones who are getting jobs are getting them because their certificates were South African certificates.*

Other people simply say that while education is a good thing because it teaches vital skills like literacy, they realise that a school-leaving certificate is no longer an insurance against unemployment.

A recurrent theme in the reasons given for the importance of male initiation was that the uninitiated were not accepted by initiates and so were at a disadvantage, particularly in the workplace. "Children should go for initiation so that they can mix with initiated people" said one mother, while another noted that "even when they're at work, the uninitiated are not welcome amongst the initiated men. If there is an accident in the mountains [at the initiation lodge] then an uninitiated policeman cannot go there".

In other words, a boy who is both school-educated and initiated maximises his opportunities in the job market — for he will be able to work with initiated men, will be strong and healthy from having been through the ordeals of initiation and will have the skills of literacy. Parents also commented that even if their children did not learn much in Transkeian schools, initiation at least would make them tough and give them 'rough' hands that would enable them to do manual labour. For the boys themselves, initiation offers them a chance to be 'real men' in an environment which generally does not give young men much of an opportunity to live out the role of the man as breadwinner and supporter of the family. Mayer (1971) also found that in the urban environment initiation (known as 'bush school') was regarded as being complementary to formal schooling and also that uninitiated boys experienced difficulties in the workplace where they were often obliged to be separated from initiated men. However, Mayer's account does illustrate that not only is the form of male initiation in the urban setting undergoing certain changes, but also that people's views as to the justification for its continuance reflect a large degree of ambivalence.

Mayer also suggests (p. 18) that decisions regarding the continuance or change of 'traditional' rites come about, to a great extent, as a result of conscious decisions on the part of actors. In St. Paul's, villagers themselves explained the renewed enthusiasm for initiation in terms of the changing attitude of the church, particularly the Anglican Church. Older residents recalled how from the 1920s onwards, the Anglican Church had taken a strict line against initiation. Initiates (of both sexes) and their parents were not permitted to take Holy Communion for six months after initiations had taken place. During the 1930s, it was said that a local Anglican priest had placed a black canopy in the church under which initiates and their parents were obliged to sit when they first returned to church. "This was taken very seriously by people, this was not a light thing" said one old man, and in fact fear of being alienated from the church and thus not being given a Christian burial is still felt very keenly amongst St. Paul's Christians (cf. Chapter Six below).

However, in recent years there has been a shift in attitude in the local churches. During the 1970s and early '80s, the local Anglican priest was himself an initiated man who regarded the practice with approval. The Catholic mission at Hardenberg also softened its approach and even runs its own initiation 'school' for boys. The youths stay at the mission for a month during which time they are circumcised by a biomedical doctor and are given Christian instruction upon the responsibilities of adult life. Young men who have been to 'real' Basotho (or Xhosa) initiation lodges, refer to this Christian initiation with the utmost disdain and contempt saying that this is not a true initiation — for the boys are 'nursed', given nice food and soft beds to sleep in — and therefore are not made into 'real men'. As for the members and leaders of the African independent churches, many stated that part of their appeal was that they are a lot more 'free' than the other churches, allowing people to practise their own customs without criticism and even including aspects like prayer for ancestors within church services. (West, 1975:178-186 describes the significance of this aspect in his study of African independent churches in Soweto.)

Today, Christianity, schooling and initiation are viewed as being complementary. Initiation rites are now usually held in the December school holidays instead of in winter and last for one month instead of three, so they do not interfere with school curricula. As I have pointed out above, the churches' attitude toward initiation appears to have become more flexible in recent years and viewed against a backdrop of rising unemployment, queues of work-seekers outside the TEBA offices, retrenchments on South African mines and in industry, the enthusiasm for boys' initiation is not so surprising.

Initiation too, I discovered, was used as an important badge of cultural distinction, for when people wanted to accentuate the ethnic differences between Basotho and Xhosa, they would often point to discrepancies in initiation practice. Xhosas would complain that Basotho send their sons to be initiated at too young an age — "how can little children be men?" they would ask. In turn Basotho would refer with distaste to the wild and rough behaviour of Xhosa initiates which they said was sanctioned. Initiation was one of the foremost examples given when people wished to enumerate cultural differences amongst themselves and often these differences seemed very minor to an outsider. Gaborieau (1985) in outlining some of the features of the Hindu-Muslim conflict in South Asia, points out that in situations of confrontation, people seek out areas of religious and cultural difference and lay stress on them — "[A]ctual features of each religion or even made up symbols are arbitrarily picked up to show that no conciliation is possible . . ." (1985:9).

Initiation rites in St. Paul's often served this purpose for they are large public events and constitute a body of customary practice wherein people can pick out significant areas of discrepancy in procedure. In addition, President Matanzima had, a short while previously, made some widely publicised speeches (broadcast on the Xhosa radio service) in which he exhorted Transkeians to follow and maintain their 'traditional' practices. Initiation thus provides people with a readily identifiable ethnic badge by which they can differentiate themselves. As real and potential ethnic tensions develop in St. Paul's (as described in Chapter Four) they provide more reasons for the persistence and growth of male initiation practices. In Port Elizabeth, Mayer found "frequent reference to initiation as an 'African' custom, distinct from White custom", he goes on to point out that "[I]n the appropriate situation the same people may be interested in the (rather minor) differences between the Xhosa and Fingo initiation" (1971:15).

The Revival of Female Initiation

In order to discuss female initiation there must be a change of emphasis, since we are not discussing the persistence of a customary practice, but rather — as I shall show — its revival. Murray (1980:125) writes that female initiation is still carried out in parts of Lesotho and Hammond-Tooke (1981) describes the rite of passage amongst the contemporary Kgaga. However, bearing in mind the necessity not to divorce such occurrences from the broader political and social context, the question is — why should Transkeian villagers, in the mid-1980s, choose to revive female initiation rites?

Since the establishment of St. Paul's in 1969/70 no female initiation rites or celebrations had ever taken place within the village and informants spoke only of two such events in the vicinity in recent memory. One was an initiation rite attended by some girls from St. Paul's which took place in 1973 in a village some 10 kms away, and the other, which was not attended by St. Paul's girls, was held at Sibi's location. These appear to have been isolated occurrences. So it is not surprising that when a number of girls from St. Paul's attended an initiation school in Sibi's location and part of the 'coming out' ceremony was held within St. Paul's itself, the event aroused a lot of interest and discussion amongst villagers. Indeed, the most public and colourful occasion that took place during my stay in St. Paul's was the return of the **ditswejane** (initiated girls) to the village.

Thirteen young women ranging in ages from 16 to mid-20s had attended the initiation school at a village in nearby Sibi's location (see maps 2 and 3) for just over a month. During this period they had been living in a shelter situated just outside the village and had been working on the field belonging to Mr Matolong — the sponsor (he was referred to as 'the owner of the initiation'). I visited the **bale** (name given to the girls during the initiation period) at this time and was allowed to watch them working and dancing. They were smeared with white clay, wore only a simple blanket fastened under their arms and when strangers approached lowered grass and bead masks to hide their faces. The **bale** also carried two sticks, one of which had two small prongs at the top and was tucked into their blankets behind one shoulder.

All men and uninitiated women (the latter known as mathisa) were required to pay a tribute (**tshwedi**) — of silver — preferably money, although pins and safety pins were acceptable — in order to come anywhere near the **bale**. Any unwary male or **lethisa** wandering near the area where the **bale** were working was in danger of being caught and beaten up.

The girls had an instructor — **Mama bale** — wife of the sponsor who, together with her assistant, taught the girls various dances and songs as well as instructing them in practical agricultural and household tasks. In the privacy of the initiation shelter, topics relating to sexual behaviour were discussed and it was said that the initiates undergo an operation whereby the ends of the genital labia are cut off. **Ditswejane** are not supposed to discuss these things with **mathisa**, but at the time of the initiation, it was a very popular topic of conversation in female circles. Although it was supposed to be a secret, most **mathisa** seemed to know about this aspect of initiation.

Five of the 13 initiates were from St. Paul's village and so it was arranged that part of their 'coming out' celebrations should be held in St. Paul's. A feast was held at Sibi's after the girls came out of their shelter, and were washed of their white clay, smeared with red oxide and dressed in the clothes of **ditswejane**. Mr Matolong, the sponsor, slaughtered an ox on the following day and the girls' parents attended the feast. They each took a sheep and **jwala** to Mr Matolong as well as a fee — R5 for each girl whose parents had sent her and R10 for each girl who had run away to be initiated. (The extra R5 constituted a kind of 'late enrolment fee' to make up for the cost of fuel already collected by the other initiates prior to their entering the lodge.)

All of the **ditswejane** and their families arrived in St. Paul's two days later accompanied by their teachers and three girls who had been initiated in 1982. These three, dancing energetically and swinging their hide skirts, preceded the procession which was surrounded by a substantial crowd of onlookers.

Mr Motaung, father of two of the newly initiated girls, slaughtered an ox that evening and the **ditswejane** and their teachers stayed in one of his rondavels and on the following day the feast was held. When Mrs Mokoena and I arrived, the street outside Mr Motaung's house was crowded with spectators waiting for the girls to appear. They were rewarded about mid-morning when the girls emerged glistening with red oxide, each wearing a **sebuthu** (an open fronted skirt made from ox-hide) over a **thethana** (a short bead skirt). In addition each wore beads on her head, wrists, neck and waist and their hair had been shaved all round the perimeter. All the girls were bare-breasted with the exception of the two married women who wore red tee-shirts. The **ditswejane** then lined up outside the house for all to see. The purpose of this display, I was told, was to give men the opportunity to choose prospective wives. If a man does choose a girl on such an occasion, then he is supposed to place a new blanket over her shoulders and give her some money, but no matches were made on this particular day.

Mr Motaung was planning to be the 'owner of the initiation' the following year when his third daughter was to be initiated. The shelter would be built in his yard and the girls would work in his field. He is the father of four daughters, and although he does have sons from a previous marriage, they belong to his ex-wife's family and were initiated by them. He said that he had been planning and preparing for his daughters' initiations for some time and this was one of the first things that he had seen to after his retirement. Mr Motaung spent most of his working-life working for the South African Railways and now lives off a Railways' pension which he says is very comfortable. During these early months of his retirement Mr Motaung began to make quite an impact on the village community. He had already hosted a 'coming out' feast for one of the boys' initiations, and in addition made himself very visible at any village functions. He always attended and contributed to the **dipitso**, was a member of the school committee, a member of TNIP and just before I left the village, he was appointed as the new village headman.

Mr Motaung probably recognises both the prestige value and commercial value of being the 'owner of the initiation'. For not only does one receive a sheep, mealie meal and a fee from the parents of each initiate, but the **bale** also work on one's field during their period of instruction. It is logical then that Mr Motaung would be keen to promote the revival of the practice of female initiation rites, just as businessmen might be keen to promote a fashion which they recognise as having lucrative potential.

The girls' initiation was certainly something new in St. Paul's. Only 16 women in the village acknowledged that they had been initiated and five of these attended the initiation just described. Thirteen of these women were under 27 years of age, whilst the remaining three were over 55, further evidence that female initiation has not been practised in the area for some time. Two of these current five initiates were the daughters of Mr Motaung, and one girl was the daughter of a woman who had herself been for initiation. The remaining two both had girl-friends in the village who had been initiated. The previous occasion that girls from St. Paul's had been initiated was in 1973, but no celebrations had been held in the village. Most village women said that their mothers had not been initiated either, and that it was a practice that they associated with their grandmothers' generation. It is clear, therefore, that there has been a discontinuity in practice of these rites. It is also interesting to note, though it is by no means conclusive, that **Mama bale** herself, whilst keen to explain the significance and meaning of various aspects of the ritual, was largely unable to do so. Of more significance is the fact that the ritual dress associated with initiation — the masks, skirts and bead-work — is very difficult to come by as these items are not generally made any more. Often long distances have to be travelled in order to find someone who still has a knowledge of these skills and then large sums of money have to be paid. One parent told me that he had spent over R120 on these items, and another said that the **thethana** alone cost R45 and that she had had to travel to the other end of the district to get it.

Within the next few years female initiations could become popular again amongst the local community, as the more girls who are initiated now, the more pressure will be upon **mathisa** to go for initiation. For the initiated girls are supposed to regard their uninitiated friends with contempt and taunt them with their inadequacies, hinting especially at their own superior sexuality. A young woman friend of mine who had not been initiated commented that she had never thought of initiation before, but now, after having seen the girls coming back, she was going to ask her husband if she could go. She also added that she did not like being mocked because she was a **lethisa**. The father of one of the initiates spoke positively about the revival of girls' rites saying —

> *Initiation is important for girls because the older people were living like that and now they can share secrets with the other women . . . it's good that people should go back to their customs. When my daughter ran away for initiation I was cross because I hadn't expected it, but then I remembered that all of the senior women in my family are initiated. So then I cooled down . . . now at Sibi's they are pressing for it to become a law [that girls should be initiated].*

However, in the main a great deal of scorn and revulsion was expressed by uninitiated women on the subject and initiation of women was often referred to as 'uncivilised' —

> *I don't like it for girls at all — it's a custom for heathens — it's something from our old forefathers — we have forgotten about them and don't believe in it any more.*

> *Our daughters would go mad if they went for initiation.*

> *I'm against this custom for girls — it was thrown away a long time ago. What's the use of it?*

Nevertheless, many women agreed that men find initiated women more sexually desirable and thus more attractive as marriage partners. Some older women cited this as one of their objections to female initiation saying that — "they like sex too much when they get initiated". It is interesting that two of the initiates were married women who had come to the initiation with the approval of their husbands. (Unfortunately, being a woman myself meant that I could not comfortably broach this topic in male company.) Possibly the idea that initiated girls are more sexually attractive and therefore prized as marriage partners could contribute to a growing popularity of the practice amongst the girls themselves. For as was outlined in Chapter One, access to a cash income is a prerequisite for successful agricultural activity and given limited employment opportunities for women, marriage remains an important means of access to cash earnings.

Lincoln (1981) in a study of women's initiation rites, points out that interpretation and analysis of ritual must take cognisance of materialistic elements as well as the more 'romantic' and 'cosmic' explanations. The idea that certain individuals — ranging from the women themselves to the organisers of initiation schools — benefit in material terms, is not inconsistent with the the notion that such rituals imbue participants' lives with special meaning.

From both perspectives, it is useful to ascertain who actually organises and carries out the initiation rituals. Lincoln suggests that if men initiate women, then the rite must be seen as one in which men enforce the subjugation and repression of women. Female initiation thus becomes a means of indoctrinating and dominating women and consolidating power and authority over them. Conversely, if women are the main agents in female initiation then the ritual can be seen as "a rite of solidarity, in which women set themselves apart from men, affirming themselves and their differences from the males around them" (1981:92). However, as Lincoln's examples and the Matatiele example illustrate, both sexes play a significant role in the initiation rite, thus exhibiting both the "repressive force of men" and "the support of . . . fellow women" (1981:93).

In the Matatiele case, it was clear that although women themselves were in charge of the actual instruction of the girls, it was men who organised and sponsored the event. Apart from the direct income and prestige that Mr Motaung and Mr Matolong may have derived from being involved in the initiation, we need once again to recognise the background factors of high migrancy rates and rising unemployment. Both of these have a significant impact upon the status of men. For most men on the South African rural periphery, success entails getting a job in one of the industrial centres and thus being away from home for up to eleven months a year. Being away from one's wife and children for such long periods engenders feelings of insecurity and inadequacy, often leading men to feel that they have lost authority and control in family matters. Reynolds (1984) examines the difficulties that male migrants working in Cape Town experience in fulfilling their roles as husbands and especially as fathers. She suggests that Black men in South Africa thus experience this separation as an additional form of poverty and deprivation. However, let us consider the alternative, where men remain in the rural areas because they cannot find jobs. These men are either unemployed or else working locally for very poor remuneration. Within St. Paul's the attitude of young women when discussing such men was often quite derisive. For instance, women friends of mine would point out certain men as being sexually impotent, accompanying such observations with a great deal of laughter and graphic descriptions of such men's inadequacies. And during my stay in St. Paul's, five cases of women physically assaulting husbands or lovers came before the village **pitso**.

These kinds of pressures, I would suggest, provide explanations for both a continued and growing support for male initiation:male as well as an interest in the revival of women's rites. Male initiation does at least provide boys with some kind of status, while female initiation would appear to provide men with a possible avenue whereby they might re-assert lost controls over women. It is interesting to note that apart from the parents of girls who had already been initiated, seven parents in St. Paul's said that they would like their daughters to be initiated. Of these seven parents, six were men.

Rituals themselves, comments Lincoln, do not "shape the way in which people live so much as they shape the way people understand the lives they would lead in any event" (1981:107). An important function of initiation, informants stressed, was that of instruction — boys were **taught** to be "real men". Female initiates spent long hours working in Mr Matolong's fields and for the rest, learned special songs and dances and received instruction on matters regarding sexuality. However, girls did not learn any practical agricultural skills that they would not have learned in the normal course of events and presumably the same could be said of the male initiates. Lincoln suggests that what such rituals do achieve, is to imbue mundane duties and drudgery with special meaning. "Such a sense of meaning is the greatest benefit that any ritual can bestow, and it is the ultimate function of all ritual to invest life with a deeper meaning than animal survival" (1981:108).

Such a claim holds even greater currency when viewed against the feelings of political alienation and marginality evident in St. Paul's. Most St. Paul's villagers feel estranged from and dissatisfied with local government which they characterise as being ineffective and oppressive. "Alienation from authorities" observes Gamson (1968:56) "means that they are regarded as incompetent and stupid in achieving collective goals and biased against the group in handling conflicts of interest. They are antiagents of the group, the agents of groups with conflicting goals." Greenberg (1974) suggests that poor people who occupy a position of political marginality react to their situation in one of three ways (or a combination of all three). When dissatisfaction with government policy is very high and is coupled with a sense of impotence and ineffectiveness, then people may (1) seek to alter the political system by violence; (2) seek to reinforce their own cultural values and in so doing, minimise contact with and ignore the local government system; (3) sink into hopeless inactivity and despair.

This kind of definition is very systematic and formulaic and is thus not altogether satisfying. However, by viewing the situation in St. Paul's from the individual's perspective, we can see that involvement in cultural activities like initiation, whilst not necessarily being a conscious or unconscious response to political alienation, is often the most satisfying course to take in a context of powerlessness and marginality. For local political activity, by necessity, is played out in the village on a very personal and individual level. Political institutions, as Gamson points out, are viewed as being either irrelevant or hostile, but minor positions of power like that of the village headman or school committee member or village ranger are vitally important. For these people wield power over such things as the collection of fuel and water and the maintenance and erection of village fences and school classrooms, issues of great significance in a community whose main concerns are usually focussed on questions of subsistence. In this instance, the sponsoring of initiation schools by certain individuals is a way of gaining popularity, prestige and influence within the village, and anybody who has influence on village affairs is bound to be approached with 'gifts' in anticipation of help. All of the 'owners of the initiation' that I met, both inside and outside St. Paul's, were men of some wealth and standing within their villages: for example, one was a headman, another a ranger, and then there was Mr Motaung, who was fast on his way to becoming a headman. Hosting initiation feasts seemed to be a means of consolidating and perpetuating their influence. Likewise for the young initiates themselves, the rite gives them a certain status which is perceived as being advantageous for their advancement in life (for a parallel cf. Mc Allister, 1981 on the subject of ritual beer drinking).

There were other bodies of custom and tradition that were often as much the focus of attention and discussion in the village as were initiation rites. Feasts to propitiate the ancestors were held frequently during my stay. People used to note with nostalgia how in the old days when somebody slaughtered an animal for the ancestors, then everybody in the village and in surrounding areas was invited and all were welcome. This may or may not have been the case, but certainly many villagers referred to the past when people practised their customs, as a 'golden age' when the crops were more plentiful and there was no sickness. Murray (1980b) describes how his informants in a village in northern Lesotho complained that it did not rain any more as it did in days gone by. Official records show that this is not the case, but rather that agricultural output has declined and people are no longer able to feed themselves. However the claim that it does not rain any more was seen as a result of people having abandoned their traditions —

> One explanation was that "the Basotho of today no longer respect the **balimo** [ancestors]" and that all boys no longer go through initiation as they did in the past. . . . [T]he . . . view expresses nostalgia for a past that offers Basotho today a merely vicarious experience of a glorious tradition (1980b:66).

Very similar views were expressed by St. Paul's villagers — past prosperity was linked to the fact that people used to uphold their customs, and initiation, in particular, was credited with ensuring the health and wealth of a past generation —

> The people of olden days could stay here in one place getting old because they were wealthy and had plenty of cattle. My father never worked in the city, he never even saw a train. Things have changed now — young people don't want to follow their own customs — they want nice clothes and nice things and they can only buy them in Jo'burg. In these days young men don't go for initiation, they don't want to buy cattle any more, now they buy tape recorders. The first thing that we used to buy was a horse and saddle and then cattle so that we could marry.

Nostalgia for a lost 'golden age' is described by West (1971) and Whisson (1972) where both found that their informants had created a mythology of the past and attributed contemporary misfortune to malevolent outside powers. The "malevolent outside power" as far as St. Paul's villagers are concerned, is the Transkeian government; and, as was pointed out in Chapter Three, the blame for the passing of the 'good old days' of White rule is laid at the door of the Matanzima regime. So I would like to argue that while it is difficult to demonstrate that Transkeian 'independence' has had the effect of increasing the occurrence of such customary practices as initiation, it has provided a context whereby these practices can gain new significance and popularity. This state of affairs was not necessarily concomitant with the change of status to 'independence', but needs to be seen as part of the ongoing situation of impoverishment that characterises the Transkeian rural areas. In addition, the proximity of a village like St. Paul's to the prosperity of Matatiele town places people in an invidious situation. Villagers are constantly being exposed to advertising campaigns and the pressures of consumerism, and they aspire to the kind of lifestyle portrayed in the local shops and demonstrated in the living habits of the White population of the town. The problem is that the more comfortable and luxurious living conditions are only within the reach of very few families in the village and for the rest, emulating the 'Western lifestyle' is beyond their financial capacities. So the failure to achieve certain status symbols, like a cement-brick house with corrugated iron roof, kitchen units, radiogram, etc. is usually compensated for by the often expressed attitude that at least people have their customs. Said one man who had a certain vested interest in maintaining enthusiasm for things 'traditional' because he had just returned to the village to practise as a **ngaka** (traditional healer) —

> *We Blacks like to take the customs of other tribes like the Whites. The problem is that we start a thing but cannot finish it. For example, the Whites have ceilings and heaters in their houses. We are stupid because we start the thing but don't know how to finish it — we build 'tin' houses without ceilings and then we* **braai** *in summer and freeze in winter. People are stupid — they just want to copy a thing without knowing how to do it properly. Like copying fashions in clothes.*

As with initiation, people often explained that abandoning their heritage and customs has led to the current increased incidence of illness and mortality in the area —

> *People should follow their own customs, if they lose their customs then they will lose their lives. Like when the child is born to a Mosotho, we make many customs — we kill a sheep to welcome the child and to make it healthy. The reason there is so much sickness is because people have lost their customs.*

> *My sons will follow the custom of initiation. People who lose their customs get confused in their heads — that's why there are so many mad people here.*

Another man who is a leader of one of the local independent churches was of the opinion that God likes people who practise their own customs —

> *The person who loses his customs stops being alive. People who copy the* **lekgoa** *customs and abandon their own are lost.*

However, it must be stressed that villagers in St. Paul's do not make a choice between a 'traditional' lifestyle and a 'Western' one; there is no division between 'red' people and 'school' people, no strict dichotomy as is presented in Mayer's work (cf. 1961). People simply live lives that are an inevitable mixture of a number of elements and at this particular time it appears that the idea of promoting certain aspects of a 'traditional' lifestyle holds particular currency.

Ritual Murder and Witchcraft Accusation

There is another dimension to the situation as well, for the fact that people have less and less faith in the local political system and are particularly sceptical about the local police force, has created a context wherein certain 'traditional' practices such as ritual murder have tended to increase. Ritual murder — **diretlo** or **bebebe** (the local slang term) refers to the killing of individuals in order to obtain human flesh for the making of powerful medicines. It is believed that these murders are usually carried out by successful people — usually businessmen — who desire to consolidate their wealth and power and to this end require flesh which must be cut from the still living victim. It was often whispered about some of the more prominent members of the area that they had reached their positions by virtue of having committed **bebebe**.

Here again it should be stressed that the revival of a rite like ritual murder cannot be viewed in a political vacuum. The dramatic upsurge of such murders in Lesotho during the 1940s is a case in point. The murders came about as a result of tensions and conflicts caused by legislation designed to curb the proliferation of Petty Chiefs and headmen. New laws meant that only chiefs and headmen whose names were officially gazetted were recognized. The right to include or remove names from the gazette was vested in the Principal Chiefs, the result being that Petty Chiefs and headmen endeavoured to do everything within their power to keep in the favour of their Principal Chiefs and competition for power led to a veritable "plague" of ritual murders (cf. Jingoes, 1975:180ff; Lye and Murray, 1981:82-84). It is clear that the undermining of the security of the lesser chiefs was the prime reason for the resurgence of these murders. Jingoes sums up the situation as follows —

> *The Chiefs were scared, and they seemed to follow each other in these ritual murders; they were almost like a fashion. I knew then, and I know now, that these murders were caused by the Proclamations. The Chiefs were not wicked or bad men: they were insecure men, who turned to the supernatural in an attempt to resist losing their rights (1975:190).*

The subject of ritual murder came under the spotlight in St. Paul's as a result of an incident just outside the village when a woman narrowly escaped becoming a murder victim (at least this was how the incident was interpreted by many villagers including the woman herself). The woman — Mrs Thamahane — went to collect firewood one evening accompanied by four women friends. (Firewood was often collected from the grazing area immediately across the road from the village.) It was twilight and Mrs Thamahane had become separated from her companions when suddenly she was confronted by a man threatening her with a knife. He accused her of stealing firewood and when she denied this he grabbed hold of her saying that he was going to take her to his friends and that the end of her life had come. At this point Mrs Thamahane had begun praying aloud and it seems that her captor lost his nerve and allowed her to escape. Quite a long time had elapsed however, so that her worried friends had already returned to St. Paul's and organised a search party. Mrs Thamahane fortunately was unscathed apart from suffering from shock, but the incident was known by almost everyone in the village by daybreak and caused a minor wave of panic amongst some of my neighbours.

For several weeks afterwards, people kept coming around to warn Mrs Mokoena and myself not to walk through the fields where the maize was high or to go anywhere at night for fear of attack. For there was almost complete unanimity of opinion that Mrs Thamahane had narrowly escaped becoming a ritual murder victim. Conversations would then often turn to gruesome reminiscences about ritual murders carried out in the area in the recent past and speculations as to the identity of the perpetrators. Once more villagers tended to perceive a direct connection between the advent of 'independence' and an increase in the number of ritual murders. They claimed that **bebebe** had not happened so much in the past, especially in Matatiele, rather it was a practice associated with Lesotho. One woman who said that she herself had also once narrowly escaped becoming a victim, recalled that **bebebe** had only happened a couple of times during her childhood, but that since the mid 1960s there had been a distinct increase and since 'independence' it had happened "too much" —

> *Since 1963 [the year of Transkeian self-government] the Whites started not to have power and it became difficult to report [crimes to the police]. The ones who do get arrested are those who are trying to help themselves to pay taxes by selling* **jwala**. *For the ones who make* **bebebe** *they get arrested and are only kept for a month and then released. It's because people who make* **bebebe** *are rich and can bribe . . . people who make* **jwala** *are poor.*

That people regarded ritual murder as a real threat was evidenced by the fact that after Mrs Thamahane's attack people walked kilometres out of their way in order to avoid passing fields or woods where assailants might be hiding, and parents would warn their children not to play in the houses of people who they suspected of having committed the crime in the past. Fear is definitely exacerbated by the belief that the police, instead of protecting the public from murderers and punishing them when they are caught, do not care about the safety of the public and are often in league with the murderers if and when they are caught. People's perceptions of the callousness of the police are illustrated by this story which was told in public at a TNIP meeting —

> *I have told you about the policemen who did not do their duty on Wednesday, and it was not only that Wednesday — they are usually that way — they are so cheeky to people. The policemen who are working are those who were trained by the South African Police. All these who were trained in Transkei do not want to do their duty — they are not well trained . . . One day my cousin's son was beaten up. We rushed to the telephone and asked the policemen to come quickly with the van. They said that their van was not an ambulance. The mother of the man was screaming but fortunately I called a taxi that was passing near the road and I took that injured man in the taxi and the one who had injured him. Immediately when we came to Maluti the man died. Who has worked as a policeman? Am I paid for what I have done or are they paid for what I have done? The criminal procedure is not used at all, we are complaining.*

It is not possible to state here categorically that ritual murder has increased since Transkeian 'independence', for not only are records extremely difficult to come by, but there is a problem in the classification of such crimes, which may just as easily be labelled as murder or mishap. Suffice it to say, many villagers were adamant that there has been an increase in these kinds of murders and it makes sense to consider that ritual murders which are supposed to give the perpetrators greater wealth and power, could be on the increase in a community in which there is both a high degree of poverty, and of inefficiency in the police force. In 1982, a ritual murder was committed in nearby Qacha's Nek, by a group of well-to-do shopkeepers who were subsequently convicted and sentenced to death (pers. comm. Qacha's Nek Medical Officer). The point needs to be made that these murders have been reported in the area in recent times and, as problems like impoverishment and ethnic and political tensions grow, so the scene is set for incidences — real or imagined — of ritual murder.

The same context gives rise to accusations — made in the 'traditional' idiom — that witchcraft and sorcery are used by local politicians as a means of jockeying for power. This they do by besmirching the name and reputation of certain of their opponents. However, in recent years this tactic has lost the impact that it probably used to have. At one of the TNIP meetings a police informer in a nearby village complained about not being able to have those people arrested who pronounce curses on others. He did not get very far with his proposal, being told that "there is no charge for cursing . . . and the chiefs should not discuss cases of witchcraft". (The Witchcraft Suppression Act, of 1957 and the Witchcraft Suppression Amendment Act, of 1970 make accusations of witchcraft a punishable offence.)

The St. Paul's police informer and former headman, Mr Melato, found a way around this obstacle by using one of two tactics. Those women whom he perceived as posing a threat to his political progress he had arrested under the charge of brewing illegal beer. Many women in the village brew **jwala**, a beer made from fermented corn or sorghum, the manufacture and sale of which is permitted within the law, and for many this is their only source of income. However, some make a more potent brew called **qorellane** or 'quick brew' the main ingredients of which are brown bread and yeast. The production of this beer and other variations on this recipe, is against the law, but it is a well known fact that **qorellane** is available in all the villages and it appears that on the whole the authorities turn a 'blind eye' to its manufacture and sale. The midnight arrests of seven St. Paul's women (the majority of whom brewed only the permitted **jwala**) served to demonstrate Mr Melato's power in general, and to warn off some of the women who were involved in the school committee and village **dipitso** in particular. Said one of the women —

> *I was arrested because Mr Melato hates me. He hates me because when there were elections for him to be headman in St. Paul's I opposed the choice at the* **pitso** *saying that he was a bad man. When the people said that they didn't want him, the chief came. At this second* **pitso** *no women were allowed to come as the majority of them were against Mr Melato. The chief talked the men into accepting Mr Melato . . . soon after that the police came at midnight and broke my door down . . .*

Another of the arrested women, who was subsequently convicted and imprisoned for two months, commented that —

> *Somebody here in the village told the police. This 'gentleman' used to seem to be kind, but really he is an enemy. There hasn't been any trouble since — maybe they don't listen to him so much at Maluti. Even if he does tell the police I won't stop, because this is how I survive. He hates a lot of people and when he was headman last time he used to send the police to arrest many people. The reason that he was headman was because he wasn't chosen by the people, but by the chief. He hates my husband and has publicly accused him of being a* **moloi** *(wizard or witch). He reported him at Maluti saying that he was using his toilet at night!*

Mr Melato's other method of dealing with his 'enemies', which more closely approximates witchcraft accusation, was having people arrested under the charge of being 'communists'. His main rival was the man who held the post of headman for most of the time that I was in St.Paul's. Even during this period Mr Melato did his best to discredit Mr Khumalo by constantly reporting him to the authorities at Maluti and accusing him of having contravened one law or other or of not meting out justice at the village **dipitso**. Mr Melato had his finest moment in 1980 when he managed to have Mr Khumalo arrested and detained for three months, during which time he was taken to Umtata and questioned about his 'anti-TNIP' activities. Mr Khumalo observed that he did not understand why he was arrested especially in view of the fact that he was an important office holder in the local TNIP branch at the time. Mr Melato, however, was quite clear in his reasoning when I questioned him, saying —

> *Mr Khumalo and his two friends have been working against the government since 1978. They were plotting against my life. They say that I am selling them to the government because I am working with the government . . . All three of them are communists because they are working against the government and break the government's laws, that's what we call people like that who speak ill of the government in public and teach others their bad ways. Mr Khumalo was put in jail in 1980 for three months for speaking ill of the government in public at the* **pitso.** *But because he had some mental disturbance . . . they let him out on the grounds of insanity. Mr Skosana [another former headman] was also put in jail for four days in 1980 for speaking against the government— he was swearing in public and speaking English.*

Mr Melato himself — who also claimed to be a **ngaka** (although it was notable that no one in the village ever consulted him) — was also accused by many of being a **moloi.** One of his close relatives put the blame for her protracted and undiagnosed illness on Mr Melato's '.i.witchcraft;' and sent her son and daughter-in-law to Swaziland to consult a famous diviner on her behalf. The diviner confirmed her suspicions and promised to counter Mr Melato's evil when her fee of R250 was paid in full. Villagers who disliked Mr Melato — and he had many enemies — would lower their voices and refer with a knowing nod to the **moloi,** while others would simply attribute his behaviour to madness.

Conclusion

What I have tried to show here is the way that people practise and uphold certain customs which have significance and utility for them in the particular context of 'independent' Transkei in the 1980s. My aim has been to illustrate how the mixture of both sentiment and environmental pressures (like poverty and political powerlessness) have served to make the continuing and even revived practice of some traditions an important dimension of village life. There is no **single** reason, I would suggest, why boys' and girls' initiations should be increasing in popularity at this time, but rather a multitude of factors some of which I have endeavoured to outline above. What I should like to emphasise, however, is that these activities do not represent some blind and conservative adherence to a forgotten and outmoded lifestyle. That people should use the idiom of custom is not so surprising, for the ideas of continuity, identity and tradition are always emotionally very powerful, and this is especially true amongst people who feel that they have very few avenues of meaningful self expression. Finally, the practical circumstances under which people are obliged to live, leads to a situation where the more unpleasant aspects of so-called tradition — like ritual murder and witchcraft accusation — are also free to proliferate.

CHAPTER 6

CONSEQUENCES OF POWERLESSNESS

In this chapter I would like to highlight a theme which has been emerging throughout this book, and that is the way that powerlessness perpetuates itself, contributing to feelings of fear, as well as to apathy, passivity and non-action. This was one of the areas where my outsider's perspective contrasted sharply with that of my informants. I would often feel very frustrated and even angry at people's reluctance to complain about some of the gross injustices that were perpetrated against them (some instances of which are described below). It did not take me long to realise that frequently there was, in fact, little that villagers could do in the face of wide-scale corruption and inefficiency. However, there were instances when it seemed clear to **me** that collective action was possible and that channels were available whereby villagers' grievances could be resolved. Unfortunately, though, experiences of the past years — some of which I have written about in the preceding chapters — have schooled people into expecting only the worst kinds of response from the authorities. The fear of becoming involved in even the mildest form of protest stems from people's powerlessness **and** from their **perceptions** of their own impotence. Often these perceptions act as self-censoring devices, which is what I am trying to convey by saying that powerlessness perpetuates itself. The belief that some Black people have of themselves — that they are inferior to Whites — contributes to their own repression, as does this belief in their own powerlessness.

I am not trying to suggest here that St. Paul's villagers are inherently passive or are incapable of standing up for themselves, just as I was not trying to suggest in Chapter Three that they **are** inferior to Whites. Nevertheless, the circumstances in which villagers live, contribute towards a general atmosphere of inertia and fear of involvement. It is my contention that this fear often surpasses the actual practical realities that people believe will necessarily follow any non-conformist actions of resistance or even complaint. In this way the fear itself acts as a constraint upon behaviour.

The research of Haines et al (1984) in Transkei highlights this very problem, pointing out particularly the way in which chiefs and headmen wield their power as allocators of land in order to control their subjects. The competition for scarce resources (particularly land, and as I have discussed above — with relation to the bureaucracy — for such things as pensions and even passports) encourages a situation where individualism is practised at the expense of communal action

(1984:16). This in turn leads to a state of affairs where people are loath to complain or question for fear of being branded as trouble-makers. However, as Haines and colleagues (1984:18) point out, these fears are not without justification —

> A fear of the authorities is not without foundation. Chiefs are served by a number of informers (kin, hangers on etc.) and appear to have links with the security police. Nevertheless there appears to be a considerable discrepancy between the actual and imagined capacity and willingness of the state (whether the tribal authorities or the higher echelons of government) to carry out punitive or coercive measures.

They also comment that lack of technical know-how as to the workings of the bureaucracy and judiciary contribute to the passivity of rural Transkeians as does the "brute reality of poverty itself" (1984:18-21). This was certainly corroborated by my experience — hardly a day went by without someone visiting me with the purpose of eliciting information as to how to go about applying for a pension or a disability grant or a plot. Once a woman even came to enquire from me the best way to go about successfully bribing the clerks at the Maluti magistrate's offices and another sought advice on how to bribe the recruiting officers at the TEBA offices. Mrs Mokoena, with her wide network of contacts and her know-how, was also constantly being requested to speak on behalf of friends and neighbours whenever she went to Maluti.

It was true also that day-to-day activities like fetching water and fuel, tending to gardens and fields, looking after children and trying to run a household all occupy and exhaust most villagers, thereby leaving them with little energy or inclination for involvement in local political activity. Moll (1983:40-42) refers to the "extra-ordinary 'passivity'" of rural women especially in light of the fact that they carry the burden of most of the work in the rural household. However, as he himself points out, this workload tends to concentrate women's energies and struggles within the sphere of the household rather than towards participation in the broader political arena.

'Justice' at the Village Pitso

I hardly need to reiterate at this point that there are few facets of village life that are not affected by the bribery that characterises so many of the formal transactions made by rural Transkeians. As I mentioned earlier, villagers claim that even **dipitso** are subject to bribery, and that it is the rule rather than the exception that 'justice' favours those who have brought gifts to the headman. In one instance this took an interesting turn when the headman refused to judge against a woman who had assaulted her mother-in-law (see Chapter Two above) because the latter had not paid various levies and contributions for village projects. Said the headman —

We shall never solve your problem here in the **pitso** *because you did not pay the money for the clinic, you are not a member of the TNIP — you haven't paid — your name is not there in the register. For the gifts for the big TNIP meetings to buy Matanzima a present — your name is not there. You did not pay any money for the* **morena** *— three times we were asking for money for him to make a feast for him after he became chief. Then there is the R1 for the dipping tank. If the people who are still owing are murdered or attacked—I' ll never solve the problem unless they pay all these amounts.*

To this, the headman's adviser added that he "appreciated" it when murders and rapes happened to those who had not paid their dues so that "they will learn the lesson that they are nowhere"!

It was the opinion of a number of my women friends that in this particular case the daughter-in-law had bribed the headman, as they claimed that it was clear to everyone that she was in the wrong. This was often the conclusion briberythat was reached by those who attended the **dipitso**. It must be noted that often the numbers were very small — usually in the region of about 45 people — as many villagers said that the **dipitso** were a waste of time. However, a core group of 'regulars' always attended these gatherings — primarily comprising the headman and his advisory committee, the village ranger, leading members of the school committee and of the local TNIP branch committee. These people were always the most vocal and the most active participants in the discussions and deliberations and even after initial disagreement, they eventually tended to support one another. As I have pointed out elsewhere, these people have — or are perceived to have — varying degrees of power within the village context. So although not many of them can actually provide access to resources (for example, the headmen must give permission to collect firewood from certain places), many do have the power to get others into trouble. They have this power either by virtue of their office, for instance the village ranger or his deputy may — or may not — report people who let their livestock stray into the fields; or because they are seen to have connections with the 'high rank' people at Maluti (Xhosa speakers may fall into this category — see Chapter Four). This is contrasted with the perception amongst ordinary villagers that they themselves have no power and that their complaints only serve to worsen their position. These points are illustrated by the following episode.

In one case that came before the village **pitso** the deputy ranger insisted on pressing charges at Maluti against a woman who had opened the water tank in order to retrieve the door key that she had accidentally dropped into it. The woman admitted that she had been in the wrong but explained that the hour had been late and that she had not been able to find the deputy ranger in order to get permission to open the tank. Despite the minor nature of the offence (the woman had not even managed to reach her key) the headman supported the deputy ranger. These two men were friends and both had reasons for taking a hard line in this particular **pitso** case. The headman, for his part, had a longstanding grudge against the woman's mother which apparently dated from a dispute with her deceased husband. The deputy ranger, on the other hand, was keen to re-establish his ascendancy after having been humiliated at the **pitso** three weeks previously. Complaints had been levelled against him that he was always drunk and that despite the fact that he earned a government salary he never saw to his duty of fixing the village fences. A complaint was subsequently made at Maluti and the man had received an official warning. Informants told me that they had made complaints before but that as a result of bribery the deputy ranger always kept his job and was only ever warned.

A common pattern for the **dipitso** is illustrated by the following case which was officiated over by the headman's adviser, Mr Ramoshebi, as the headman was away for the day. About 50 people were present when Lebetla, a young man from a neighbouring village, laid a charge against his wife. His wife had left him and returned to her family in St. Paul's, taking his trunk with all his clothes, blankets and radio with her. The young man had discovered this only when he had returned home from working on the mines in the Transvaal, and now he was requesting the return of his belongings. It was evident from early on in the proceedings that Mr Ramoshebi was not at all well disposed towards Lebetla, who was constantly harangued and insulted and accused of being a liar. He was charged with not supporting his wife and with not having completed paying bridewealth for her. He was then asked why he had not come to ask for his wife to return to him and if he did want her back, why he had not supported her properly. In the end the young man was thoroughly cowed and confused, and the issue of his belongings was hardly discussed at all. Eventually Mr Ramoshebi ruled that Lebetla could get his things, on condition that he paid R60 to his wife's family to compensate them for having supported her during the past months, despite the fact that Lebetla insisted that he had been sending money home.

Apart from the fact that Lebetla was harrassed throughout the **pitso** and often not given a fair opportunity to defend himself, it might seem at first sight that justice was indeed done. After all, it is not uncommon that migrants, for one reason or another, are unable to send money home and a woman may have little recourse but to seek help from her family. However, as the **pitso** broke up and people drifted back to the activities of their daily routine, many villagers were grumbling angrily that there was "no truth" at the **pitso**. Upon questioning them further, I discovered what was apparently common knowledge in the village — that Lebetla's wife had left her husband for another man whom she had already 'married'. Furthermore, it was agreed that Lebetla was a good man who had been supporting his wife well and that Mr Ramoshebi had been bribed. When I asked why no one had mentioned this and spoken up in defense of Lebetla, the reply was — "the people of the **pitso** would be against you and you would never have a chance if your case came up before them". Haines et al refer to similar case material of their own and point out the important role that fear itself plays in controlling people. They too note that —

A fear of voicing one's grievances, of questioning or speaking against tribal authorities is a pervasive sentiment. "By complaining you create enmity", a Qumbu resident remarked. "We cannot complain." (Haines et al, 1984:17).

Once drawn into a network of bribery and corruption — existing in the first place because of a scarcity of resources over which there is limited control — resistance becomes very difficult. Although villagers complained about bribery, many conceded that they had themselves paid bribes and Haines et al comment that this participation lends legitimacy to the 'system' and reinforces the habit of silence. We must recognise too, how the pursuit of the individual's interests, which may be as straight-forward as simply staying out of trouble, serves to divide people and diffuse potential communal resistance.

Corruption in the Church

As I have pointed out already, villagers **do** have reason to fear the authorities — even officials at the bottom of the hierarchy, like headmen — as these people are able to wield varying degrees of power over them. However, fear and powerlessness are such all-pervasive features of village life, that individuals who are completely outside of the government structures, are able to play on the same emotions within the community. The malpractices that are carried out in many of the local churches are indicative of this. The corruption which takes place within some of the churches in many ways mirrors that which occurs in everyday practice in other spheres of life. People's responses to it are also very similar, in that many officials can count on silence from their congregations rather than angry complaints. For the fear of complaining and getting involved runs so deep, that the same attitudes and behaviour of non-involvement that were displayed at the **dipitso** can also be observed in the face of the most blatant church corruption.

It had not been my intention originally to investigate in any detail problems related to the church. However, during my stay in St. Paul's, the significance of church membership and the distress that church corruption caused, were increasingly pressed upon my attention. In fact, I eventually became reluctantly involved in one particular controversy concerning a local priest.

About six months before my stay in St. Paul's, Mr Ndlaleni came to take up office as priest at the St. Paul's Anglican mission. As head of the parish, 20 stations (churches), scattered throughout the district, came under his jurisdiction, although the church where his main duties lay, was at St. Paul's. Mr Ndlaleni and his alleged activities proved to be such a major topic of local gossip, that like it or not, I was obliged to take notice of him.

Mr Ndlaleni, like many other people in official positions with whom I came into contact in Transkei, used his power and authority to his own material advantage. As we have seen, villagers have, over the years, come to accept this kind of conduct as normal. Even in the church a certain amount of corruption is tolerated almost without comment, because priests, like civil servants, do perform certain services. Chief amongst these is the performance of Christian burials, which as many clerics have successfully impressed upon the minds of their congregations, are an essential prerequisite for entry into the kingdom of heaven. Ensuring a church burial is generally achieved by maintaining church membership during one's life-time, and this is commonly done by paying a nominal annual membership fee (usually in the region of 60 cents per adult and half-price for children). This system is very open to abuse because some priests, hungry for church funds — either for improving church buildings, etc. and thus adding to their own prestige, or for their own private use — threaten parishioners with hell-fire if they do not pay their membership fees. This is why church membership cards are commonly called 'tickets to heaven', and are valued as such. An elderly widow told me that she had originally been an Anglican, but with marriage converted to Presbyterianism. She reflected that she really preferred the Anglican Church, but did not want to change again because "I am old and might die any day and then I would lose my Presbyterian seat in heaven and might not get an Anglican one".

Sixty cents per person per year might sound like a trifling sum, but for a large family with little or no cash income, those few rands a year may constitute a substantial amount, especially when several years' backlog of subscriptions are also due. Priests also ask their congregations to contribute various sums for church projects, and they may also ask for money for themselves as their stipends are very modest (in the region of R400 per month at the time of writing).

Mr Ndlaleni got off to a bad start with his congregation because of his inability to speak Sesotho. A shortage of priests had obliged the church to employ a Xhosa-speaker from outside of the area. Unfortunately, Mr Ndlaleni was opposed to the idea of one of his lay preachers acting as interpreter, and was reported to have voiced the opinion that the people should learn Xhosa. This kind of approach became the hallmark of Mr·Ndlaleni's ministry, together with his enthusiasm for the collection of church funds. One long-standing church member said of him —

> He's only interested in **nqunquthela** [a Xhosa word literally meaning a drive or joint effort, here referring to fund raising collections in church which are usually accompanied by singing and carried out in a festive mood]. Mr Ndlaleni said that he is not interested in copper money which he says is 'black money'. Even the ordinary collection starts with five cents and if there are a lot of five cent pieces he gets very angry. He likes paper money the best.

> Last week when he visited the church at P. he just stood by the door and said bring the money here. The preacher gave him the money and then he left without even giving a service. Those people were very unhappy and dissatisfied.

There was a definite difference of degree between Mr Ndlaleni and other priests who set great store by the collection plate. Perhaps realising the extent of the vulnerability and submissiveness of his congregation, he rapidly began to increase his demands and commit various excesses. It was alleged that he abused a woman in the church, actually hitting her, whilst berating her for the raggedness of her clothes. When reproached by one of the lay preachers, who later recounted the story to me, Mr Ndlaleni said that he had not hit the woman, but had merely "pulled" her because she was "dirty". Standards of dress were apparently high on his list of priorities. He demanded that women should not wear 'Sotho dress' (meaning popular 'German print' cottons and blankets) to church. Rather they should come in **makgoa** clothes, and instead of wearing shawls and blankets in winter, should buy overcoats, which, conveniently enough, they could purchase from Mrs Ndlaleni who hawked clothing in her spare time. He insisted that the members of the church women's club change the colour of their uniforms, involving them in considerable expense, and shouted at any woman who came to church in her old uniform.

Every week disgruntled parishioners would regale me with the latest Ndlaleni outrage. He expected people to labour in his garden (which was bigger than the regular-sized gardens of the villagers), refused to visit the sick and dying unless he was brought a letter of 'referral' from the appropriate lay preacher, swore at people in the church if displeased with the quality of their singing. He became more and more insistent in his demands for money —

> *Last time the priest demanded R4 from everyone who wasn't going to the big* **nqunquthela** *in Kokstad; R2 from the harvest — even from those who don't have a field or a garden; R2 from the spouse of the harvester. High rank people should pay R5 each. Fifty cents to buy new windows for the church; R1 for being a member of the women's club; 50c to buy soap for the priest's wife; 50c from each member to sympathise for his child who died; 20c for his sister who died.*

All the time these requests were backed by threats of hellfire and damnation — for his power lay in his ability to refuse church burials and baptisms and therefore deprive people of their 'seats' in heaven. One man told me how Mr Ndlaleni had asked him why he did not attend church services more regularly and the man explained that when his grandchildren were away, he had to stay at home and look after his goats as they were the source of his livelihood. The priest replied that he would not be able to bury him when he was dead — he would have to let his goats take him to heaven. Mr Ndlaleni made it quite clear to his congregation that anyone who died without having paid for all of their tickets or who had not attended church regularly (thereby helping to fill the collection plate) would not be buried by him or any of his lay preachers.

These threats were not without substance. Soon after his arrival he scandalised many people by refusing to bury a prominent church member, who was reputed to have been a generous and charitable man and supporter of the church. Mr Ndlaleni claimed that the man had not been a regular church-goer and so refused to bury him, standing his ground in this case as he did with a number of others. Similarly, he 'persuaded' women to attend choir practice regularly by suggesting that otherwise their children would not be eligible for baptism. On one occasion he was even reported to have said that if women were prevented from coming to choir practice by husbands or sick children, then he would pray for them to die in order to remove their interference.

I have included this lengthy account of Mr Ndlaleni's activities (which is by no means exhaustive) in order to show just how far he was able to go. During the course of the year, attendance at his church dropped, with people usually turning to the various independent churches. They proved a popular choice, particularly because many of their preachers were willing to bury anyone's dead at short notice (including those refused burial by Mr Ndlaleni), and also because many of these churches did not have a system of tickets or membership fees. As one convert explained —

> In this Apostolic church I can pray for my ancestors, in Mr Ndlaleni's church I had to pay to make a special prayer for them. We do pay tickets — 20c a year, but no one is forced and no one is refused burial for not paying. They have got no objection to any person who is created by God and they will help bury them. They will bury someone if Mr Ndlaleni refuses to do so.

Nevertheless, a lot of people were unhappy at the thought of leaving the church which they had attended all their lives and which, in many cases, their families had belonged to for generations. Often when my friends complained about Mr Ndlaleni I would ask them why they did not want to join another church. Usually people would reply that their forefathers had helped build the church and that it was nearby, so why should they walk long distances to go to a church that was foreign to them? A fair enough response certainly, but why was it that Mr Ndlaleni was able to continue his corrupt ministry unhindered for so long? And why was it that at the time of my census, despite Mr Ndlaleni, a majority of St. Paul's villagers declared Anglican membership?

At this point chief Ramohlakoana's role in the establishment of the St. Paul's mission should be recalled as well as the positive part played by the Anglican Church authorities on behalf of the local people at the time of the sale of Wallace Farm (see Chapter One). It is reasonable to assume that these factors would account, to some extent, for a loyalty to the Anglican Church. However, it would also be naive to disregard the significance and power of Ndlaleni's threat to jeopardise an individual's entry into heaven. As Geertz points out, religious beliefs constitute a kind of reality for the people who hold them. He defines religion as —

> *a system of symbols which acts to establish powerful, pervasive and long-lasting moods and motivations in men by formulating conceptions of a general order of existence and clothing these conceptions with such an aura of factuality that the moods and motivations seem uniquely realistic (1966:4).*

Thus the necessity of having 'tickets to heaven' cannot be brushed aside as something which is simply untrue and — maybe in the eyes of the outsider — rather ridiculous. Crapanzano (1980:23) warns against the "presumption of our collapsing the real and the true" and points out that we need to question the status of 'reality'. We need to recognise in this case that ". . . men's notions, however implicit, of the 'really real' and the dispositions that these notions induce in them, **color their sense of the reasonable, the practical, the humane and the moral**" (Geertz, 1966:41, my emphasis).

If we accept the reality of people's beliefs in heaven and hell as well as their beliefs in the crucial role of church membership in attaining seats in heaven (not to do so is surely to be guilty of a kind of gross ethnocentricism), then we can understand the reality of Mr Ndlaleni's power. However, as I have pointed out elsewhere with reference to local government, people were in no doubt that such power was being abused. They were also convinced of their powerlessness to change the situation. In actual fact a few members of the congregation — lay preachers — had tried to complain about their priest some months previously. Their efforts were thwarted, however, because the letter of complaint was directed to Mr Ndlaleni's superior in the church hierarchy who, unfortunately, happened to be one of his friends and the person who had helped to secure him the job. The complaint, therefore, did not have the desired effect and in fact was shown to Mr Ndlaleni who then publicly denounced the signatories, commending their souls to the devil. This explained the resigned attitude of those who continued to go to the church: there simply appeared to be no solution to the problem. The parallels are obvious — people face corruption in the bureaucracy on a daily basis, they learn to be frightened to talk 'politics' and they learn that complaint through the 'proper channels' is usually fruitless (cf. Chapter Three above). Lack of confidence, know-how and communal organisation all contribute to powerlessness and vulnerability.

It was at this point that I became personally involved in the matter. A priest from a neighbouring parish, with whom I had discussed the problem, asked me to intervene, as church ethics prevented him from doing so himself. He suggested that I write a letter of complaint and get as many people as possible to sign it. He would then take the letter to someone higher up in the church hierarchy, so bypassing Mr Ndlaleni's immediate superior and also guaranteeing the anonymity of the signatories. I was thus faced with a problem that many researchers have to deal with when in the field — should I interfere or should I mind my own business? Hatch (1983), in discussing the problems raised by cultural relativism, suggests a point at which tolerance should be suspended and interference justified. "What . . . makes tolerance so difficult to defend is the use of unmistakable, unmitigated coercion ... Tolerance should not extend to actions and institutions in which coercion is used against human beings" (1983:95-6). As far as I was concerned, Mr Ndlaleni **was** using coercion against his congregation, and so, in consultation with Mrs Mokoena (herself a member of the church), I decided to go ahead with the priest's suggestion.

With the help of Mrs Mokoena and other church members I drafted a letter, but difficulties arose when it came to persuading people to sign it. Not many wanted to run the risk — despite the promise of anonymity — of being 'found out' by Mr Ndlaleni and then hearing themselves damned in church. As it turned out, their fears were well founded. The letter was indeed taken straight to the top church authority, but from there it was simply referred to the attention of Mr Ndlaleni's friend and superior, with exactly the same results as the time before. By this time I was back home in Cape Town and wondering if, after all, I should have minded my own business. The matter was eventually resolved many months after I had left St. Paul's. Investigation procedures were finally instigated by the church authorities and at the time of a return visit to the village in September, 1985, I learned that Mr Ndlaleni had been transferred elsewhere. On the Sunday following his departure the church was reported to be full once more.

I have given this account of extortion in the local church in order to show how the resignation and fear, that often characterise villagers' dealings with representatives of the local government, have carried over into other aspects of life which have nothing to do with the government. Mr Ndlaleni was able to intimidate his congregation simply by playing on their fear and counting on their powerlessness. It is not possible to dismiss the congregation's lack of action by saying that the issue was not really important to them. For, as I have tried to show, church burials and the associated salvation that they promise **are** important to many people and in order to attain this ultimate goal, one needs to be baptised and confirmed and be a church member. This is quite apart from the clubs, like the women's club and the youth club, that normally provide opportunities for socialising and relaxation. One may say that after the first letter of complaint there was little that the congregation could do to remove Mr Ndlaleni. On the other hand, the priest met with very little active resistance, and many people did continue to attend church, which presumably encouraged him to greater and greater excesses.

The Usurpation of the St. Paul's Headmanship

An episode with much the same characteristics as the Ndlaleni affair, took place in St. Paul's during my stay. In Chapters One and Five, I have briefly described the animosity between Mr Melato and Mr Khumalo which had, at one time, resulted in Mr Khumalo's arrest. When I arrived in the village, Mr Khumalo was headman, much to the chagrin of Mr Melato who was of the opinion that — "he should be sent to jail, because he's a crazy communist". To this end he expended a great deal of effort travelling back and forth reporting Mr Khumalo at the Tribal Authority and at Maluti. For example, Mr Khumalo had to face a charge at the Tribal Authority **pitso** that he was illegally allowing villagers to cut firewood from a nearby plantation. Mr Melato lost the case, but remained undeterred.

With the 'election' of the new chief at Ramohlakoana (cf. Chapter One above) Mr Melato saw his chance to oust his rival. He had manoeuvered himself into a position of influence over the simple and impressionable chief Teboho. This became fully evident at a general meeting at Ramohlakoana, called in order for the new chief to address the people. After Teboho had been introduced, he greeted us all, advised people to bring their problems to him and told us that Mr Melato was going to speak on his behalf, whereupon he sat down and said nothing for the rest of the meeting. Mr Melato then proceeded to tell those assembled that the chief wanted new headmen and he read out a list of names for the different villages. When he came to St. Paul's he read out the name of Mr Lerole, a man who was rarely involved in village politics, and added that he, Mr Melato, would be the 'second' — a position not accorded to any of the other villages. Someone in the audience asked — "Morena is working for us — yes — but why is he demoting headmen? Why does he want new people?" Mr Melato's reply was — "Ask the government. The government wants new people . . . the government is our God, and in the Bible it says we should obey God".

In the weeks that followed it became clear not only that Mr Melato had no intention of being a 'second', but also that Mr Lerole did not want to be headman. Thereafter, Mr Melato set about making his 'authority' felt with a series of demands which outraged many villagers. A number of people in the village owned tractors which provided them with a source of income. During the agricultural season they were hired out for ploughing and later on for bringing home the harvest. At other times villagers paid tractor-owners for fetching large containers of river-water for washing, sand for building and firewood. Mr Melato sought to put a stop to this by insisting that people had no right simply to take sand, water and wood which belonged not to them, but to the Transkeian government. He demanded, instead, that **he** be paid by the tractor owners for these raw materials or else he would report them at Maluti. He also intimated that he would have women who were brewing illegal beer arrested, and he told me that he was going to make sure that communists were put behind bars.

It began to look as if Mr Melato had established himself as headman and was set to make and enforce his own rules for St. Paul's. People were frightened of him — in the past he had organised arrests and it was whispered that he was a wizard, or at the very least, that he was mad. Again people were outraged but said they were too scared to go to the local authorities for fear of reprisal from Mr Melato. However, opposition and intervention did materialise a few weeks later in the person of Mrs Mokoena, who as a tractor-owner, was particularly keen to rid the village of Mr Melato's influence.

The experience which preceded her action, should, I think, be briefly described. After I had been in St. Paul's for four months, Mrs Mokoena accompanied me to

Cape Town for a holiday and to attend a conference — the Second Carnegie Inquiry into Poverty and Development. Mrs Mokoena attended a number of the sessions dealing with rural development, and one of the themes which emerged was the need for people in villages to organise themselves in order to achieve collective action. Accounts of the successes that rural villagers had had in organising projects in various parts of the country made a deep impression on her. In addition, she and I obviously spent a great deal of time discussing village affairs and possible solutions to problems. Upon our return to St. Paul's, Mrs Mokoena persuaded a group of women friends to accompany her to the police station at Maluti, where they reported Mr Melato. Apparently, the authorities had been completely oblivious of his activities and of his self-appointed position. Furthermore, the group was told that the police were rather exasperated with Mr Melato's constant reports and that in future they would not be taking much notice of him. The following day he was summoned to Maluti and reprimanded, and thereafter Mr Motaung was installed in the village as the new headman (see Chapter Five).

I have to stress here that, modest as it may sound, the episode described above constituted the only organised act of resistance that I witnessed during my six months in St. Paul's. In this instance, Mrs Mokoena, spurred by her recent experience outside the confines of the village, as well as by personal interest, was able to convince her friends that by acting together they could be strong. The common thread that runs through the two cases described above, is the need for individuals who not only have leadership and organisational ability, but who also have a working knowledge of local government structures.

The Lack of Organised Resistance

It should be noted at this point that writers usually tend to examine instances of resistance rather than the lack thereof, action rather than non-action. The point was made in the Introduction that those who wield power need the active or **passive** support of a public and therefore it is important to document and explain cases of non-action just as it is for the more obvious instances of active resistance. In Transkei there have been instances of rural rebellion — in Pondoland in 1960 and Tembuland in 1962-1963 — which have been extremely well documented (see for example, Mbeki, 1964; Southall, 1983:108-114; Lodge, 1983:279-289). It is worth looking at these instances of resistance very briefly in order to see if they can inform us about the lack of resistance in contemporary St. Paul's.

Lodge comments that these revolts were centred around very localised conflicts and were thus largely parochial in character. The upheavals and loss of land and stock which were attendant upon the implementation of 'betterment' schemes were the main causes for complaint. This situation, coupled with the existence of very powerful local authorities (especially in Pondoland), who were particularly corrupt, provided the key ingredients for revolt. In the case of the Pondo rebellion, Lodge also points out the degree of participation of young men of working age —

migrant workers — who happened to be at home at the time as a result of a temporary slump in the sugar industry. The fact that these uprisings were centred around dissatisfaction with land rehabilitation is important. Up until 1965 it can be contended that agricultural activities provided a substantial contribution toward household subsistence and that 'betterment' often implied a very real loss of income. However —

> *the resilience of rural reaction depended on the survival of at least a residual peasant mode of production. By the mid-1960s, under the impact of the state rural resettlement policies (the average rural population doubled between 1955 and 1969), even a caricature of this had disappeared in many parts of the countryside (Lodge, 1983:290).*

Lodge's comments about these events in the early '60s highlight some important areas of focus when discussing St. Paul's. Firstly, as was described in Chapter One, 'betterment' took place in St. Paul's in 1969 and was not characterised by the kinds of hardship that was often the case in other areas. Furthermore, only 52% of village households have a field and amongst these households agricultural activities provide only a contribution to subsistence needs. Land rehabilitiation has thus never been an issue of **common grievance** with villagers and even the current agricultural scheme affects only a small proportion of St. Paul's residents. As mentioned above, one of the striking features of a system characterised by bribery and corruption is its divisiveness — people tend to compete with one another by engaging in the system rather than uniting.

An important characteristic of the causes for the Pondo resistance was the "particularly repressive chieftaincy" (Southall, 1983:108). There was evidence in Matatiele which showed that in certain instances villagers could only be pushed so far and no further (as was the case to some extent with Mr Melato). In a village, about 15 kms from St. Paul's, an incident took place which became widely known and talked about in the district. The village police informer had apparently been conducting a reign of terror. Not only did he inform on people against whom he held personal grudges, but he also arrested individuals **himself** on whom, it was alleged, he carried out grim tortures, like hanging them upside down and mutilating them with pliers. This carried on for months without the informer either being reported or harmed in any way, until one day he voiced his intention of reporting a group of village youths, who, he said, were dealing in dagga. However, the man never reached Maluti; his body was found in a ditch with its throat cut. Mass arrests were made in the village, and for days after the incident, people were seen walking on the main road past St. Paul's, after having been released from questioning. Eventually everybody was released and no charges were laid for the killing. Although this may appear to be a successful case of resistance, the following points need to be made: Firstly, the man had been committing violent excesses for many months, during which time he remained completely unscathed. Secondly, his eventual murder was not an organised act of defiance, but probably a spontaneous act of self-preservation by a threatened group of individuals. Moll points out that in Transkei, when it did take place, "political and economic protest . . . acquired a distinctive conservative and bucolic bias rarely overcome by rural organisation" (1983:40).

It should be noted, however, that cases of resistance have been reported in several schools in the Matatiele district (see Rietstein, 1982). Events in South Africa, particularly since 1976, have shown that young people are increasingly in the forefront of resistance struggles. Even in the Pondoland rebellion, Lodge emphasises the important part played by young working men. This point has important implications for St. Paul's village where there is a preponderance of women, old people and young people **who have never been employed.** Possible reasons for the 'passivity' of rural women have already been discussed, but what of the large number of younger residents? It should be stressed that very few youths from St.Paul's actually attend high schools and it is in the high schools that most of the strikes have taken place. Furthermore, rising unemployment has meant that many young people have never been to work in towns and so have had little direct contact with the centres of resistance struggles in South Africa. All of the factors described above contribute to the situation whereby —

> *Black rural communities are peculiarly isolated by vast distances, by the reserve system, and systematic barriers controlling the flow of people and ideas between town and countryside (Lodge, 1983:290).*

A dictionary definition of 'repression' suggests that it is — the state in which people are kept under, put down or where thoughts are banished to the unconscious (Chambers Twentieth Century Dictionary). The degree to which this definition held true for St. Paul's villagers was very striking. I would argue that one of the major stumbling blocks to organising effective resistance is the marked lack of political consciousness amongst the people. Given the ingredients of poverty, powerlessness and fear it is not surprising that, to date, cases of resistance have been few and far between.

CHAPTER 7

CONCLUSION

In Chapter Six I looked specifically at the issue of powerlessness and discussed the lack of organised resistance to local instances of corruption and extortion. Real and potential divisions and disunity have, in fact, been recurring themes throughout this book. St. Paul's is, as yet, fairly free of overt manifestations of division and violence, for the main lines of antagonism and resentment appear to be drawn between the 'seniors' — particularly the local representatives of the Transkeian government — and the ordinary villagers. I have tried to show that while there is a range of economic differentiation within St. Paul's, the local Transkeian elite is not really represented in the village save for a tiny minority of relatively wealthy individuals. However, given the context of limited resources (for example, new sites), the issue of ethnicity would seem to provide a fertile ground in which animosities and divisions could proliferate in the future.

Many of the hardships and problems described by St. Paul's villagers are features of every-day life in the South African rural areas and are in no way unique to either Matatiele or Transkei. High incidences of poverty and unemployment, as well as ignorance and vulnerability are the fruits of the 'homelands' policy and the lot of many of the people who are obliged to live in these areas. It has been my intention to show how the exigencies of 'homeland' life have been exacerbated by the fact of 'independence'. For on the one hand, 'independence' **has** provided a small elite with new opportunities for the kind of 'primitive accumulation' described by Southall and others; and on the other hand, villagers perceive that their quality of life has deteriorated as a direct result of Transkei's changed status.

One of the results of the whole 'homelands' exercise has been that of dividing people and we can see how this has been particularly effective in the way that ethnic consciousness has been created and heightened. In St. Paul's we see how ethnic political divisions serve to deflect antagonisms away from White central government and towards the Transkeian regime. 'Independence' may not have brought about any radical changes to the pre-1976 situation, but in the eyes of ordinary villagers the blame for the deteriorating economic situation, rising rates of unemployment and the general hardships of rural life must be placed at the door of the Transkeian government.

The fact that St. Paul's villagers are not self-sufficient, and thus are not 'uncaptured' as Hyden suggests is the case for Tanzanian peasants, plays an important part in their own powerlessness. This, together with a local history in which there have been no instances of successful resistance struggles has contributed to the resigned attitude with which villagers view their situation. The ordinary villagers of St. Paul's do not have much leverage to bring about significant change in their own lives, especially within the system of Tribal Authorities. However, their position is further weakened through fear and self-censorship causing them to be trapped in their own web of silence. This background of frustration and fear must be taken into account when seeking explanations for the continued (and sometimes revived) enthusiasm for the practice of 'traditional' customs. For not only do such practices provide ethnic 'badges' of identity in an environment where ethnic divisions have such fertile ground in which to proliferate, but they also provide channels for self-expression in a social context where individuals have little chance of material prosperity or political expression. People's perceptions that 'independence' has worsened their position and that they were better off 'under' White rule cannot be brushed aside. For it should be stressed that these attitudes constitute reality for the people who hold them and play an important role in influencing both villagers' actions and non-actions.

As was pointed out in the Introduction, the villagers'-eye-view of life in 'independent' Transkei highlights a range of concerns not considered by researchers who have concentrated on broader 'macro' issues. Stultz (1980) suggested that Transkeian 'independence' might in time form the basis for more positive, non-violent change in southern Africa by making Whites accustomed to the notion of power-sharing or consociationalism (cf. Stultz, 1980:144-156). Southall countered this suggestion by stating that the pre-requisites for consociationalism do not exist in South Africa and that — and this is sigificant — "consociationalism generally relies upon the majority of citizens remaining relatively apolitical, all segments of South African society are now highly politicized" (1980:725).

Southall (1983) also speculated that instead of the gradual evolutionary change, suggested by Stultz (1980) and Butler et al (1977), flowing from 'homeland independence', it is more likely that the growing militant and revolutionary mood of the urban areas will spread to the countryside. He foresees this kind of popular revolt as a significant threat to the 'homeland' leaders, who he believes will be obliged to seek help from South Africa, and so leave no one in any doubt as to their collaborative role and the meaninglessness of their so-called sovereign status. He concludes finally, by stating that 'homeland independence' is extremely fragile and doomed to only a short and finite existence.

It is impossible to generalise from the case of St. Paul's to the whole of Transkei, or even to the rural areas in general. However, the evidence from the village does call into question some of the broad macro perspectives. For example, Stultz's notion that Transkei's 'half loaf' is better than nothing at all and that at least now Blacks within Transkei do not have to suffer the degradation and humiliation of apartheid, is certainly not borne out by the testimony of the majority of St. Paul's villagers. For them 'independence' has not meant an increase in dignity, or even as Stultz suggests, that their lives have remained materially unchanged. Nor have they perceived the economic and political opportunities that Butler et al see flowing in the wake of 'independence'. The ordinary villagers' view is that a handful of privileged members of the 'high rank' live in relative luxury, while their own positions have worsened since 1976. It is difficult to argue that 'independence' has brought Transkeians more self-dignity, when daily they have to face problems such as who to bribe for a pension or a work contract.

On the other hand, Southall's claim that all sections of South African society are "highly politicized" contrasts strikingly with the reality of village life in St. Paul's. Precisely because rural villagers suffer the effects of the apartheid system by being isolated, impoverished and poorly educated, they are not "politicised" in the way that Southall suggests. For repression not only manifests itself in the overt activities of those in power, but also in the consciousness of the villagers themselves. Furthermore, his speculation that the "widespread disaffection in the townships . . . may spread to the homelands themselves, and rural resistance to apartheid . . . may well take the form of direct attacks upon the bantustan leaderships and symbols of their authority" (1983:303) needs to be qualified. In St. Paul's it seems more likely that future resistance will be mobilised around very localised issues and not simply against those who are part of the corrupt system, for this constitutes the 'normal' rather than the exceptional. Instead, I would suggest, it will be manifested against those like Mr Melato and the neighbouring village police informer who go beyond the bounds of 'normal' corruption and become outrageous in their demands. At present these individuals are not viewed as being products or symbols of the apartheid system. In the same way villagers do not identify the oppression that is part of life in an 'independent homeland' as a corollary of apartheid, but place the blame on the inability of Blacks to rule themselves. It is in this manner that the 'homeland' policy succeeds in driving wedges between people and deflecting antagonism and resistance away from the real architects of the system.

BIBLIOGRAPHY

Aron, R. 1969. Two Definitions of Class, in A. Beteille, (ed): **Social Inequality. Selected Readings.** Harmondsworth: Penguin.

Ashton, H. 1952. **The Basuto.** London; Oxford University Press.

Bardsley, G. 1982. Politics and Land in Matatiele 1844-1900: A Report from the Archives, in **Social Dynamics,** 8 (2).

Barley, N. 1983. **The Innocent Anthropologist: Notes From a Mud Hut.** Harmondsworth: Penguin.

Barnes, J.A. 1968. Networks and Political Process, in M.J. Swartz, (ed): **Local Level Politics: Social and Cultural Perspectives.** Chicago: Aldine Publishing Company.

Barth, F. (ed) 1969. **Ethnic Groups and Boundaries. The Social Organization of Culture Difference.** Boston: Little Brown and Company.

Bates, R.H. 1976. **Rural Responses to Industrialization: A Study of Village Zambia.** New Haven and London: Yale University Press.

Beattie, J. 1984. Objectivity and Social Anthropology, in S.C. Brown (ed): **Objectivity and Cultural Divergence.** Cambridge: Cambridge University Press.

Berlin, I. 1976. **Vico and Herder: Two Studies in the History of Ideas.** London: The Hogarth Press.

Boonzaier, E. and Sharp, J. 1988. **South African Keywords: The Uses and Abuses of Political Concepts.** Cape Town: David Philip.

Boonzaier, E., Skalnik, P., Thornton, R., West, M. and Gordon, R. 1985. Review discussion of **Waiting: the Whites of South Africa** by V. Crapanzano, in **Social Dynamics,** 11 (2).

Buhrmann, M.V. 1984. **Living in Two Worlds: Communication Between a White Healer and her Black Counterparts.** Cape Town and Pretoria: Human and Rousseau.

Bundy, C. 1972. Emergence and Decline of a South African Peasantry, in **African Affairs,** 71.

Bundy, C. 1979. **The Rise and Fall of a South African Peasantry.** Berkeley: University of California Press.

Burgess, M.E. 1978. The Resurgence of Ethnicity: Myth or Reality?, in **Ethnic and Racial Studies,** I (3).

Butler, J., Rotberg, R.I. and Adams, J. 1977. **The Black Homelands of South Africa: The Political and Economic Development of Bophuthatswana and KwaZulu.** Berkeley and Los Angeles: University of California Press.

Carter, G.M., Karis, T. and Stultz, N.M. 1967. **South Africa's Transkei: The Politics of Domestic Colonialism.** London: Heinemann.

Charton, N. 1976. Black Elites in Transkei, in **Politikon,** 3 (2).

Clifford, J. 1983. On Ethnographic Authority, in **Representations,** 2, Spring.

Cloete, D. 1985. Maize Production Schemes in the Transkei, paper presented at the annual conference of the Association of Sociologists of Southern Africa, University of Cape Town, July, 1985.

Cohen, A. (ed). 1974a. **Urban Ethnicity**. London: Tavistock Publications.

Cohen, A. 1974b. **Two-Dimensional Man: An Essay on the Anthropology of Power and Symbolism in Complex Society**. London: Routledge and Kegan Paul.

Cohen, A. 1981. **The Politics of Elite Culture: Explorations in the Dramaturgy of Power in Modern African Society**. Berkeley and Los Angeles: University of California Press.

Comaroff, J.L. 1982. Dialectical Systems, History and Anthropology: Units of Study and Questions of Theory, in **Journal of Southern African Studies, 8** (2).

Crapanzano, V. 1980. **Tuhami: Portrait of a Moroccan**. Chicago and London: University of Chicago Press.

Davidson, B. 1961. **Black Mother: Africa and the Atlantic Slave Trade**. Harmondsworth: Penguin.

De Wet, C.J., Mc Allister, P.A. 1983. Rural Communities in Transition: A Study of the Socio-Economic and Agricultural Implications of Agricultural Betterment and Development, **Development Studies Working Paper no. 16**. Institute of Social and Economic Research, Rhodes University, Grahamstown.

Ellis-Jones, J. 1985. Transkei's Agricultural Development Strategies and the Role of the "Transkei Agricultural Corporation", paper presented to Institute of Management and Development Studies workshop on Rural Poverty and Development Strategies in Transkei. University of Transkei, April, 1985.

Elphick, R. 1983. Methodology in South African Historiography: A Defence of Idealism and Empiricism, in **Social Dynamics**, 9 (1).

Epstein, A.L. 1971. Comments on: B Magubane: A Critical Look at Indices Used in the Study of Social Change in Colonial Africa, in **Current Anthropology**, 12, (4-5).

Feyerabend, P. 1975. **Against Method: Outline of an Anarchist Theory of Knowledge**. London: Verso.

Foster,G M and Kemper, R V (eds) 1974. **Anthropologists in Cities**. Boston: Little, Brown and Company.

Gaborieau, M. 1985. The Hindu-Muslim Divide in India, in **Anthropology Today**, 1 (3).

Gamson, W.A. 1968. **Power and Discontent**. Homewood, Illinois: The Dorsey Press.

Geertz, C. 1966. Religion as a Cultural System, in M. Banton (ed): **Anthropological Approaches to the Study of Religion**. ASA Monograph no.3. London: Tavistock.

Gluckman, M. 1968. Inter-hierarchical Roles: Professional and Party Ethics in Tribal Areas in South and Central Africa, in M.J. Swartz (ed): **Local-Level**

Politics: Social and Cultural Perspectives. Chicago: Aldine Publishing Company.

Goldberg, M. 1985. Ideology as False Consciousness?, in Z. Van Straaten (ed): Ideological Beliefs in the Social Sciences. HSRC Research Report Series: 5. Pretoria: Human Sciences Research Council.

Greenberg, S.B. 1974. Politics and Poverty: Modernization and Response in Five Poor Neighbourhoods. New York: John Wiley and Sons.

Haines, R.J., Tapscott, C.P., Solinjali, S.B. and Tyali, P. 1984. The Silence of Poverty: Networks of Social Control in Rural Transkei, Carnegie Conference Paper No. 48, University of Cape Town.

Hall, R.H. 1974. Food for Nought: The Decline in Nutrition. New York: Vintage Books.

Hammond-Tooke, W.D. 1975. Command or Consensus: The Development of Transkeian Local Government. Cape Town: David Philip.

Hammond-Tooke, W.D. 1981. Boundaries and Belief. The Structure of a Sotho Worldview. Johannesburg: Witwatersrand University Press.

Hart, G.P. 1972. Some Socio-Economic Aspects of African Entrepreneurship With Particular Reference to the Transkei and Ciskei. Occasional Paper No. 16, Institute of Social and Economic Research, Rhodes University.

Hatch, E. 1983. Culture and Morality: The Relativity of Values in Anthropology. New York: Columbia University Press.

Hirson, B.C. 1977. Rural Revolt in South Africa 1937-1951, in The Societies of Southern Africa in the 19th and 20th Centuries, Vol 8. Institute of Commonwealth Studies, University of London.

Holy, L. and Stuchlik, M. 1983. Actions, Norms and Representations. Foundations of Anthropological Enquiry. Cambridge: Cambridge University Press.

Horowitz, D.L. 1975. Ethnic Identity, in N. Glazer and D.P. Moynihan (eds): Ethnicity: Theory and Experience. Harvard: Harvard University Press.

Houghton, D.H. (ed) 1952. The Keiskammahoek Rural Survey, Vol II. The Economy of a Native Reserve, D.H. Houghton and E.M. Walton. Pietermaritzburg: Shuter and Shooter.

Hyden, G. 1980. Beyond Ujamaa in Tanzania: Underdevelopment and an Uncaptured Peasantry. London: Heinemann.

Isaacs, H.R. 1975. Basic Group Identity: The Idols of the Tribe, in N. Glazer and D.P. Moynihan (eds): Ethnicity: Theory and Experience. Harvard: Harvard University Press.

Jackson, A.O. 1975. The Ethnic Composition of the Ciskei and Transkei. Pretoria: Government Printer.

James, D. 1983. The Road From Doornkop. A Case Study of Removals and Resistance. Johannesburg: South African Institute of Race Relations.

James, D. 1985. From co-operation to "co-operative": changing patterns of agricultural work in a rural village. Paper presented at the annual conference of the

Association of Sociologists of Southern Africa. University of Cape Town, July, 1985.

Janzen, J.M. 1978. **The Quest for Therapy: Medical Pluralism in Lower Zaire.** Berkeley: University of California Press.

Jingoes, S.J. 1975. **A Chief is a Chief by the People. The Autobiography of Stimela Jason Jingoes.** London: Oxford University Press.

Keesing, R. 1981. **Cultural Anthropology. A Comparative Perspective.** New York: Holt, Rhinehart and Wilson.

Kuper, A. 1980. The Man in the Study and the Man in the Field. Ethnography, theory and comparison in Social Anthropology, in **European Journal of Sociology, XXI.**

Lacey, M. 1982. Locating Employment, Relocating Unemployment in **'Homeland' Tragedy. Function and Farce.** DSG/SARS Information Publication 6, Johannesburg.

Lappé, F.M. and Collins, J. 1982. **Food First.** London: Abacus.

Laurence, P. 1976. **The Transkei: South Africa's Politics of Partition.** Johannesburg: Ravan Press.

Leatt, J. 1982. Astride Two Worlds: Religion and Values Among Black Migrant Mineworkers on South African Gold Mines in **Journal of Theology for Southern Africa,** 38.

Le Roy Ladurie, E. 1978. **Montaillou: Cathars and Catholics in a French Village, 1294-1324.** London: Scholar Press.

Lincoln, B. 1981. **Emerging From the Chrysalis. Studies in Rituals of Women's Initiation.** Cambridge, Mass. and London: Harvard University Press.

Lodge, T. 1983. **Black Politics in South Africa Since 1945.** Johannesburg: Ravan Press.

Lye, W.F. and Murray, C. 1980. **Transformations on the Highveld: The Tswana and the Southern Sotho.** Cape Town: David Philip.

Magubane, B. 1971. A Critical Look at Indices Used in the Study of Social Change in Colonial Africa, in **Current Anthropology,** 12, (4-5).

Malinowski, B. 1967. **A Diary in the Strict Sense of the Term.** London: Routledge and Kegan Paul.

Manona, C.W. 1980. Ethnic Relations in the Ciskei, in N. Charton (ed): **Ciskei: Economics and Politics of Dependence in a South African Homeland.** London: Croom Helm.

Marcus, G. and Cushman, D. 1982. Ethnographies as Texts, in **Annual Review of Anthropology,** II.

Mare, G. 1981. Old Age Pensions and the Bantustans, in **Work in Progress,** No. 17.

Marx, K. and Engels, F. 1970. **The German Ideology.** Part one with selections from parts two and three. New York: International Publishers.

Mayer, P. 1961. **Townsmen or Tribesmen: Conservatism and the Process of Urbanisation in a South African City.** Cape Town: Oxford University Press.

Mayer, P. 1971. "Traditional" Manhood Initiation in an Industrial City: The African View, in E.J. De Jager (ed): **Man: Anthropological Essays Presented to O. F. Raum.** Cape Town: C. Struik.

Mayer, P. 1980. The Origin and Decline of Two Rural Resistance Ideologies, in P. Mayer (ed): **Black Villagers in an Industrial Society. Anthropological Perspectives on Labour Migration in South Africa.** Cape Town: Oxford University Press.

Mbeki, G. 1964. **South Africa: The Peasants' Revolt.** Middlesex: Penguin.

McAllister, P.A. 1981. **Umsindleko: A Gcaleka Ritual of Incorporation.** Rhodes University Institute of Social and Economic Research, Occasional Paper Number 26.

McAllister, P.A. 1985. Agricultural "Betterment", Conservatism and Resistance to Poverty in Willowvale District. Paper presented at a workshop on Rural Poverty and Development Strategies in Transkei. Institute of Management and Development Studies, University of Transkei, April, 1985.

Moll, T. 1983. No Blade of Grass. Rural Production and State Intervention in Transkei, unpublished B.A. (Hons) dissertation, Sociology, University of Cape Town.

Molteno, F. 1977. The Historical Significance of the Bantustan Strategy, in **Social Dynamics,** 3 (2).

Muller, N.D. 1984. Results of the 1980 Transkei Census, Institute of Management and Development Studies, Transkei, Statistical Series, No. 4.

Muller, N.D. 1986. Behind the Bolted Door: Rural Poverty and Social Relations in the Transkei Bantustan, unpublished paper.

Murray, C. 1977. High Bridewealth, Migrant Labour and the Position of Women in Lesotho, in **Journal of African Law,** 21 (1).

Murray, C. 1980a. Migrant Labour and Changing Family Structure in the Rural Periphery of Southern Africa, in **Journal of Southern African Studies,** 6 (2).

Murray, C. 1980b. Sotho Fertility Symbolism, in **African Studies,** 39 (1).

Murray, C. 1981. **Families Divided. The Impact of Migrant Labour in Lesotho.** Johannesburg: Ravan.

Nelson, N. 1979. **Why Has Development Neglected Rural Women? A Review of the South Asian Literature.** Beccles and London: Pergamon Press.

Parsons, T. 1975. Some Theoretical Considerations on the Nature and Trends of Change of Ethnicity, in N. Glazer and D.P. Moynihan (eds): **Ethnicity: Theory and Experience.** Havard: Havard University Press.

Pelto, P.J. and Pelto, G.H. 1978. **Anthropological Research: The Structure of Inquiry.** Cambridge: Cambridge University Press.

Ranger, T. 1983. The Invention of Tradition in Colonial Africa, in E. Hobsbawm and T. Ranger (eds): **The Invention of Tradition.** Cambridge: Cambridge University Press.

Reitstein, J. 1982. Living and Schooling Conditions of Youth in a Transkei Village, unpublished B.A. (Hons) dissertation, Social Anthropology, University of Cape Town.

Reynolds, P. 1984. Men Without Children. Paper presented at the Second Carnegie Conference on Poverty and Development, University of Cape Town.

Rogers, B. 1980. **Divide and Rule. South Africa's Bantustans.** London: International Aid and Defence Fund.

Ross, R. 1974. The Griqua in the Politics of the Eastern Transkei, in C. Saunders and R. Derricourt (eds): **Beyond the Cape Frontier: Studies in the History of the Transkei and Ciskei.** London: Longman.

Ross, R. 1976. **Adam Kok's Griquas: A Study in the Development of Stratification in South Africa.** Cambridge: Cambridge University Press.

Ryan, A. 1985. Marx, History, Science and Social Science, in Z. Van Straaten (ed): **Ideological Beliefs in the Social Sciences.** HSRC Research Report Series: 5. Pretoria: Human Sciences Research Council.

Saunders, C. 1974. The Annexation of the Transkei, in C. Saunders and R. Derricourt (eds): **Beyond the Cape Frontier: Studies in the History of the Transkei and Ciskei.** London: Longman.

Segar, J. 1982. Food and Health-Care in a Betterment Village, unpublished B.A. (Hons) Dissertation, Social Anthropology, University of Cape Town.

Segar, J. 1984. Social Inequality in a Transkeian Betterment Village, Carnegie Conference Paper No. 49, University of Cape Town.

Seymour-Smith, C. 1986. **MacMillan Dictionary of Anthropology.** London: MacMillan.

Sharp, J. and West, M. 1982. Dualism, Culture and Migrant Mineworkers: A Rejoinder From Anthropology, in **Journal of Theology for Southern Africa,** 39.

South African Institute of Race Relations 1979. **Survey of Race Relations in South Africa.** Johannesburg: SAIRR.

South African Institute of Race Relations 1983. **Survey of Race Relations in South Africa.** Johannesburg: SAIRR.

Southall, R. 1977. The Beneficiaries of Transkeian "Independence", in **Journal of Modern African Studies,** 15 (1).

Southall, R. 1980. New Perspectives on South Africa, in **Journal of Modern African Studies,** 18 (4).

Southall, R. 1983. **South Africa's Transkei: The Political Economy of an 'Independent' Bantustan.** New York: Monthly Review Press.

Spiegel, A.D. 1979. Migrant Labour Remittances, Rural Differentiation and the Developmental Cycle in a Lesotho Community, unpublished M.A. thesis, Social Anthropology, University of Cape Town.

Spiegel, A.D. 1982. Spinning off the Developmental Cycle: Comments on the Utility of a Concept in the Light of Data from Matatiele, Transkei, in **Social Dynamics,** 8 (2).

Spiegel, A.D. 1985. Cases from East Griqualand, in **Grahamstown Rural Committee Newsletter**, 3.

Streek, B. and Wicksteed, R. 1981. **Render Unto Kaiser. A Transkei Dossier.** Johannesburg: Ravan Press.

Stultz, N.M. 1980. **Transkei's Half Loaf: Race Separatism in South Africa.** Cape Town: David Philip.

Swartz, M.J. (ed) 1968. **Local Level Politics: Social and Cultural Perspectives.** Chicago: Aldine Publishing Company.

Tatz, C. 1962. **Shadow and Substance in South Africa: A Study in Land and Franchise Policies Affecting Africans 1910-1960.** Pietermaritzburg: University of Natal Press.

Thornton, R. 1983. Narrative Ethnography in Africa, 1850-1920: The Creation and Capture of an Appropriate Domain for Anthropology, in **Man** (N S), 18 (3).

Tötemeyer, G. 1984. Ethnicity and National Identification Within (South) Africa Context, in **Politikon**, II (1).

Vinnicombe, P. 1976. **People of the Eland. Rock Paintings of the Drakensberg Bushmen as a Reflection of their Life.** Pietermaritzburg: Natal University Press.

Weber, M. 1978. G. Roth and C. Wittich (eds): **Economy and Society: An Outline of Interpretative Sociology** Vol I. Berkeley: University of California Press.

West, M.E. 1971. **Divided Community. A Study of Social Groups and Racial Attitudes in a South African Town.** Cape Town: A.A. Balkema.

West, M.E. 1975. **Bishops and Prophets in a Black City. African Independent Churches in Soweto Johannesburg.** Cape Town: David Philip.

Whisson, M.G. 1972. **The Fairest Cape? An Account of the Coloured People in the District of Simonstown.** Pietermaritzburg: South African Institute of Race Relations.

Wilson, M. 1971. The Growth of Peasant Communities, in M. Wilson and L.M. Thompson (eds): **The Oxford History of South Africa** Vol 2. Oxford: Clarendon Press.

Yawitch, J. 1981. **Betterment, the Myth of Homeland Agriculture.** Johannesburg: South African Institute of Race Relations.

Government Publications

The East Griqualand Commission, 1879 G72-'80.

Report of the Griqualand East Commission (Vacant Lands Commission), 1884 G682E.

Other

Plan no. T922/58A, Transkei Department of Agriculture and Forestry, Maluti.

Index